The Fiscal Maze

Parliament, Government and Public Money

Alex Brazier and Vidya Ram

Hansard Society 2006

The Fiscal Maze
Parliament, Government and Public Money

Text © Hansard Society 2006
Published by the Hansard Society, 40-43 Chancery Lane, London WC2A 1JA.
Tel: 020 7438 1222, Fax: 020 7438 1229, Email: hansard@hansard.lse.ac.uk.

All rights reserved. No part of this publication may be reproduced, stored in a retrieval system, or transmitted in any form or by any means, without the prior permission of the Hansard Society.

The Hansard Society is an independent, non-partisan educational charity, which exists to promote effective parliamentary democracy.

The Hansard Society's Parliament and Government Programme works on all issues relating to the reform of Parliament, engagement between Parliament and the public and promoting effective parliamentary government through a range of conferences, publications, public and private meetings.

We set the agenda on parliamentary reform through our work with parliamentarians and others to improve the operation of parliamentary government and encourage greater accessibility and closer engagement with the public.

For information and other Hansard Society publications visit our website at **www.hansardsociety.org.uk**.

The views expressed in this publication are those of the authors. The Hansard Society, as an independent non-party organisation, is neither for nor against. The Society is, however, happy to publish these views and to invite analysis and discussion of them.

ISBN: 0 900432 08 X

Cover design by PricewaterhouseCoopers
Printed and bound in Great Britain by PCM Limited

Authors

Alex Brazier is Senior Research Fellow on the Parliament and Government Programme, Hansard Society.

Vidya Ram is Project Manager on the Parliament and Government Programme, Hansard Society.

Acknowledgements

The authors of this report are grateful to the Government and Public Sector practice at PricewaterhouseCoopers (PwC) and the Chartered Institute of Public Finance and Accountancy (CIPFA) for the generous funding for this project and to the National Audit Office for their research support. We would also like to thank a number of parliamentary staff, including Gillian Fawcett, formerly of the Scrutiny Unit, for their comments. We are very thankful to our colleagues at the Hansard Society, especially Declan McHugh, Virginia Gibbons and Clare Ettinghausen, and to members of the Hansard Society Council, particularly Kate Jenkins and Paul Evans for their input and advice throughout this project. Finally, we would like to thank all those who submitted written evidence to this inquiry, the participants at a private seminar in December 2005 and all those who were interviewed as part of this inquiry.

PwC is a leading professional services firm providing services to the public sector and is currently advising a number of major central government departments, local authorities and other public sector organisations. PwC also acts as the Audit Commission's leading private sector provider of audit services to local government and health bodies.

CIPFA is one of the leading professional accountancy bodies in the UK and the only one which specialises in the public sector. It is responsible for the education and training of professional accountants and for their regulation through the setting and monitoring of professional standards. Uniquely among the professional accountancy bodies in the UK, CIPFA has responsibility for setting accounting standards for a significant part of the economy, namely local government.

Table of Contents

Executive Summary and Main Recommendations	1
1. Introduction	6
2. Parliament's Financial Scrutiny: Goals and Aspirations	9
3. Parliamentary Scrutiny of Financial Legislation and Taxation	17
4. Parliamentary Scrutiny of Expenditure Plans	25
5. Parliamentary Scrutiny of Government Expenditure	35
6. The Role of the Audit Commission	46
7. Audit and Devolution	48
8. The Private Finance Initiative	51
9. Scrutiny of European Union Expenditure	54
10. The Role of the House of Lords	57
11. Developing Good Practice	60
12. Measuring Performance: Inputs and Outputs	66
13. Support and Resources	69
14. Connecting with the Public	72
15. Conclusion	75
Appendix 1: List of evidence received	78
Appendix 2: List of attendees at the private seminar	78
Bibliography	80

Executive Summary and Main Recommendations

Parliament's scrutiny of taxation, expenditure and public services is fundamental to our political system and to the relationship between Parliament, government and the public.

Parliament has a unique constitutional role in authorising and scrutinising government finance but the current system for financial scrutiny does not work effectively.

Parliament has a responsibility to restate and reassert its constitutional role in all aspects relating to financial scrutiny. Government has a responsibility to engage constructively with Parliament in this work. Both sides should recognise that good scrutiny makes for good government.

Parliament is uniquely placed to put pressure on government to secure openness about its activities and to press for improvement and efficiency in public services. It should institute mechanisms to ensure that this pressure is applied to get the best results possible. **Parliament could and should do more to secure a full level of openness and accountability. We hope that this report stimulates debate and encourages reform in this crucially important area. It is therefore to Parliament that we direct our options for reform and put forward recommendations for change.**

This report identifies solutions and options for reform based on two main themes. First, the mechanisms which would strengthen Parliament's ability to carry out financial scrutiny and second, the changes needed to ensure that this scrutiny work has more of an impact. Our conclusions and recommendations focus on the following areas:

Parliamentary Scrutiny of Financial Legislation and Taxation

Parliament should increase its impact on the Budget process, to secure explanation from government for its priorities and to scrutinise better the legislation that enacts government taxation proposals. The advent of the Pre-Budget Report has reduced the need for traditional Budget secrecy. The timetable for consideration of both reports by Parliament should allow for thorough parliamentary scrutiny.

- *In the period between the Pre-Budget and the main Budget, parliamentary committees should take expert and public evidence on the government's plans, make a case for the priorities it wishes government to consider, and ensure the government provides full information and explanation for its proposals. There should also be more opportunities to debate and question government spending proposals. [3.3]*

Financial legislation has not benefited from the procedural reforms which now give Parliament an opportunity to comment on and influence many draft bills.

- *The entire Finance Bill should be subject to pre-legislative scrutiny by a parliamentary committee. [3.9]*

Parliament should also improve the way that it scrutinises tax legislation and administration.

- *Alternative options for reform include: the establishment of separate Tax Administration or Taxation Committees in the House of Commons or a Joint Committee on Tax Administration. In addition, a Tax Law Commission could be established to overview the effectiveness of tax legislation and make proposals for change. [3.12]*

The Treasury Committee is overburdened and unable to scrutinise government policy and activity, most particularly in relation to scrutiny of HM Revenue and Customs (HMRC).

- *We recommend the establishment of a separate HMRC Committee in the Commons, building on the Treasury Committee's HMRC sub-committee. [3.15]*

Parliamentary Scrutiny of Expenditure Plans

When it comes to authorising government spending proposals, Parliament is seen as little more than an acquiescent bystander. On estimate days, billions of pounds of public spending are authorised without sufficient scrutiny or debate. More opportunities are needed for the House of Commons to be involved in the scrutiny of government spending plans.

- *More scrutiny of government expenditure plans should take place within parliamentary committees, particularly through consideration of Departmental Annual Reports (DARs). [4.9]*

- *Select committee reports on DARs should link to the formal processes of the House, through debates in the main chamber, to strengthen scrutiny of spending plans. [4.17]*

- *Departmental estimates should also be sent to committees at the earliest possible date so that committees have the opportunity to thoroughly examine them before they are voted on in Parliament. [4.10]*

Spending reviews provide the ideal opportunity for Parliament to scrutinise government spending plans at both the macro and micro level.

- *Parliament should become fully involved in the process leading up to the Comprehensive Spending Review (CSR) 2007 and should subject the forthcoming interim report on the CSR to detailed scrutiny. [4.14]*

Parliamentary Scrutiny of Government Expenditure

The combined work of the National Audit Office (NAO) / Public Accounts Committee (PAC) and the departmental select committees results in significant savings for government, but considerably more could be achieved. However, the fundamental question is whether long term improvements in outcomes are achieved, wider lessons are learned and mistakes not repeated.

- *There should be a move towards a deeper notion of accountability to ensure that individual lessons are translated into general reforms of public institutions that are found to be flawed. [5.12]*

There should be a more co-ordinated approach to follow up the work of the PAC.

- *The introduction of a regular trigger for review of NAO/PAC reports would mean that their recommendations were more systematically followed up. [5.13-16]*
- *DARs should also include a specific section on progress made in implementing recommendations and the outcomes of the changes made. [5.22]*

To give a higher priority to financial scrutiny within select committees, designated sub-committees should carry out a wide range of functions, including following up NAO/PAC recommendations as well as scrutinising spending plans, DARs and departmental estimates.

- *Parliament should consider piloting a Finance and Audit Sub-Committee in a number of departmental select committees. [4.18 & 5.20]*

The work of the Audit Commission should be subject to closer consideration by Parliament. Select committees should seek to forge closer relationships and make greater use of its evidence to strengthen their work.

- *We recommend that the appropriate select committees consider Audit Commission reports on a more systematic basis. [6.4]*

The Private Finance Initiative

Parliament's system of financial scrutiny must respond to changes to the system of governance in the UK, including the Private Finance Initiative (PFI).

- *PFI contracts should be subject to full select committee scrutiny and 'commercial confidentiality' should not be used to block full parliamentary scrutiny. [8.8]*

Scrutiny of European Union Expenditure

The need for better parliamentary scrutiny of European Union spending is made all the more urgent by the continuing controversy over the EU's accounts.

- *More consideration of EU spending should take place in parliamentary committees, supported by the NAO, including a greater role for the European Union Committee of the House of Lords. [9.6-9.8]*

The Role of the House of Lords

The House of Lords should play a more active role in carrying out financial scrutiny while respecting the financial precedence of the Commons. Members of the Lords have expertise and understanding that could strengthen the scrutiny work of Parliament.

- *In the area of tax administration and the follow up of PAC recommendations, further scrutiny could be conducted by the Lords. [10.4-6]*

Developing and Enhancing a Scrutiny Culture

Financial scrutiny should be considered as one of the most fundamental tasks of MPs. **The recommendations in this report will only be effective if accompanied by a greater willingness from MPs and Peers to engage in financial scrutiny work.**

Over the past few years the government has introduced a range of innovations designed to increase transparency of the financial and expenditure system, including Public Service Agreements, Whole of Government Accounts and Resource Accounting and Budgeting.

- *It is essential that Parliament responds by making full use of the information and opportunities presented by these innovations to strengthen its scrutiny work. [12.7]*

Parliament would benefit from a more systematic approach to scrutiny. It should ensure that all the different processes and procedures it adopts are suitable for the purpose for which they are intended and link together to offer a complete picture of government activity.

- *Parliament should adopt a set of best practice guidelines to ensure that its scrutiny methods are fit for purpose, comprehensive and result in improvements in government performance. Its scrutiny processes should be continually monitored and adapted if necessary. [11.5]*

The Commons Scrutiny Unit already provides valuable support to select committees.

* *We recommend that this work should be built upon, either through an expansion of its role or through its evolution into a Parliamentary Finance Office to provide comprehensive support on all financial matters to individual parliamentarians and select committees. [13.6]*

Parliament has a responsibility to the public to ensure that financial scrutiny is carried out in the public interest and reflective of their concerns.

* *Parliament should provide a document which sets out the operation of financial scrutiny which is publicly available. Where relevant, the views and experiences of members of the public and interested groups should be sought and should feed into the parliamentary process. [14.4]*

Section 1

Introduction

1.1 Public spending and taxation has a profound impact on every member of the public. Each year the government raises and spends over £500 billion of public money and the way that this takes place determines the quality of day-to-day experiences, from the medical treatment people receive in the NHS, to the provision of local bus services and the number of police on the streets.

1.2 Parliament provides the crucial link between government – and its power to take money from the public and spend it on their behalf – and the public themselves. As the public's representative body, it is Parliament's responsibility to hold government to account between elections for the money it raises and spends and it has unique constitutional functions to enable it to carry out this work. Crucially, the government must gain parliamentary approval for its spending and taxation plans. Parliament is also responsible for scrutinising future and past expenditure, holding government to account for its actions and ensuring that public money is raised and used wisely (and for appropriate purposes) and provides value for money.

1.3 Given the dependency of all forms of government activity on public finances, financial scrutiny underpins all other forms of accountability, and goes to the heart of the relationship between Parliament and government. It is therefore essential that the system functions as efficiently and effectively as possible. There is, however, much improvement that could be made in this area. The issue was previously considered by the 2001 report of the Hansard Society's Commission on Parliamentary Scrutiny, *The Challenge for Parliament, Making Government Accountable*. The report identified major flaws in the way that Parliament authorises and scrutinises government finance and identified a range of reforms that could make the current system operate more effectively.

1.4 Five years on, while many of the Commission's recommendations have been implemented, few relating to financial scrutiny have been adopted. There have been some developments: the core tasks of select committees now include considering departmental spending proposals and departments have obligations to provide them with explanatory material. The Scrutiny Unit was established in 2002 to provide specialist support, including on financial matters, to Commons select committees. Central government has fully implemented a system of Resource Accounting and Budgeting (RAB) to capture more effectively the real costs of providing services, and the powers of the NAO have been extended to include a wider range of public bodies. However, little attempt has so far been made to consider the overall picture and assess the extent to which the totality of reforms has succeeded in strengthening parliamentary scrutiny.

1.5 It is for this reason that the Hansard Society has returned to this crucial issue, with the aim of evaluating the changes that have taken place and considering what further reforms are needed. In December 2005, we produced *Inside the Counting House: A Discussion Paper on Parliamentary Scrutiny of Government Finance*. This interim paper had two distinct purposes: firstly, it provided an account of the financial scrutiny system in Parliament, designed to be accessible to those with little knowledge of the area. The complexity of the procedures involved means that there is little understanding of the system outside Parliament and government; indeed it may even be something of a mystery to many of those who operate within the system. That paper, therefore, provided an overview of the major elements of the financial scrutiny system: the way that Parliament authorises taxation and government spending (including the Budget, the Finance Bill, and the supply process), as well as the methods used to scrutinise government expenditure and public service delivery, focussing on the work of the public audit bodies, and within Parliament, on the work of the Public Accounts Committee (PAC) and other select committees.

1.6 Secondly, the briefing paper provided a preliminary analysis of the system as it currently operates, highlighting its strengths and weaknesses, as well as reforms that have taken place since 2001. It drew upon the findings of previous inquiries which had considered the issue, as well as evidence to this inquiry from a range of interested parties and experts within and outside Parliament and government.

The scope of this report

1.7 In this final report, we seek to identify solutions to some of the concerns that have been raised. The two main themes of our proposals are, firstly, which mechanisms could strengthen Parliament's ability to carry out financial scrutiny and, secondly, what can be done to ensure that this scrutiny work has more of an impact. The central objective of our proposals is that Parliament should be able to secure improved accountability from the government for the money that it spends on our behalf, and that this scrutiny work should then lead to greater efficiency and effectiveness in the public services.

1.8 Many of the options identified in this report involve procedural, structural and functional changes that would either give Parliament greater powers on matters relating to financial scrutiny, or more opportunities to carry out this work. At the same time, we identify ways in which the capacity of parliamentarians to carry out financial scrutiny could be strengthened, through the provision of better information, specialist support, or training. We look specifically at the role of independent audit and scrutiny bodies and how Parliament can make the best use of their work, and at the ways in which the work and reports of Parliament can be followed up effectively to ensure that they make an impact on the operation of government. We consider possible changes to the operation of parliamentary committees, and the role the House of Lords – which has traditionally been excluded from financial matters – could play without intruding on the financial precedence of the Commons. Beyond this, we consider how the processes could be made more accessible to a wider public. This paper also considers the scrutiny of European Union expenditure – an issue not considered in the interim paper – and how this could be strengthened. We look at the operation of financial procedures in the devolved assemblies and cite international comparisons that provide examples of best practice.

1.9 Where relevant we draw on the description of the financial scrutiny system contained in *Inside the Counting House* to underpin our analysis and proposals in this final report. We make further reference to the written evidence received as part of this project,[1] and also refer to ideas and issues raised at a private seminar held in December 2005, which brought together individuals with an interest and expertise in the area.[2] For a more detailed account of the processes of financial scrutiny, and a glossary of relevant terms, see *Inside the Counting House,* which is available (for free download) on the Hansard Society website, www.hansardsociety.org.uk .

---

[1] Appendix 1 shows the full list of evidence received. Quotations and references used in the text are from the evidence received as part of this project, unless otherwise stated.

[2] Appendix 2 shows the participants at the seminar which was held under Chatham House Rules and no comment and points raised are attributable to any individual participants.

Section 2

Parliament's Financial Scrutiny: Goals and Aspirations

2.1 In this section, we look at the nature of Parliament's financial scrutiny functions, considering what they currently achieve, and most importantly, what they could and should achieve. We look at the scope for improvement in the way that Parliament carries out this work. This section considers some of the general themes that underpin this subject before moving on, in the subsequent sections, to consider specific areas in more detail and discuss options for reform.

Parliament and government: different roles and powers

2.2 The Hansard Society promotes the case for an effective Parliament, one that has a more equitable relationship with government and which is able to affect, influence and hold government to account for its work and activities. In the field of taxation and public expenditure, government dominance over Parliament is particularly marked. When it comes to giving the government authorisation to raise and spend money Parliament is seen by many people as little more than an interested and acquiescent bystander. However, the current, markedly unbalanced relationship is not the inevitable expression of our constitutional arrangements. Parliament could do considerably more to make its mark in this area.

2.3 Financial matters go to the heart of our political system and the relationship between government and Parliament. Both Parliament and government have different roles to play. For example, the constitutional convention of the financial initiative of the crown precludes Parliament from seeking to impose taxes or grant permission for public expenditure unless it is requested by government. Therefore, government has the constitutional powers to present spending programmes to Parliament in order to exercise its mandate from the electorate and deliver the policies that it wishes to implement. It should be remembered that government is not a monolithic institution and within government the relationship between the Treasury and different departments has a significant impact on the drawing up and implementation of policies and legislation. However, while acknowledging these elements, this report considers the totality of government finance as it is put forward by government.

Parliament's input into taxation and spending

2.4 Many would argue that government uses effectively the powers and authority at its disposal to achieve its required ends in financial matters. But can the same be said of Parliament? Does it make the most of its unique constitutional position to increase its influence and make an impact on the financial plans that government proposes? In the view of many commentators, Parliament's influence over government proposals for taxation and expenditure, and priorities within that expenditure, is virtually non-existent. The essential relationship between Parliament and government is that the latter proposes and the former simply agrees. To draw an analogy, the government decides the value of the cheque, to whom it should be paid and when, and Parliament simply signs it. As we point out in section four, the UK is considered to have among the weakest systems for parliamentary control and influence over government expenditure in the developed world.

2.5 The nature of the relationship between Parliament and government in the UK when it comes to spending and taxation issues is often contrasted unfavourably with that in other countries. In particular, the example of the United States is frequently cited, where Congress has much greater negotiating ability and budgets and financial legislation are frequently batted between the executive and the legislature. One participant at our seminar commented: 'I used to salivate listening to the powers of US Congressional Committees where you get junior deputy assistant secretaries coming before the relevant appropriation sub committee to try and justify expenditure and how people at the committee had 20 years experience on the issue.' There is a view that the UK should strive towards something approximating the American system. However, this is unlikely to happen: to achieve this Parliament would have to be given much greater power on appropriation decisions and this is something that most governments would not be interested in doing. Moreover, some would argue that such reform is neither desirable nor realistic within our system. From this viewpoint, there are advantages to having our current structure of fiscal policy – in the hands of the executive – without any protracted negotiation between the executive and legislature and from committee to committee. The US system is not without its critics, who point to instances where departmental activity has been brought to a standstill when funding has not been granted on time. In addition, given the crucial importance of spending to the government's ability to carry out its programme of work, any changes towards this model would fundamentally alter the relationship between Parliament and government. Furthermore, supporters of the UK system point out that our current arrangements provide certainty and stability and allow for clear lines of responsibility about the decisions made and who takes them. **But even if the essential architecture of our system were not changed, there are many ways that Parliament could significantly improve its scrutiny of government, secure greater explanation and transparency from government and ensure that it builds a more influential and equitable relationship with government based on a deeper notion of accountability.**

2.6 Of course, the UK system is, and very likely will remain, fundamentally different from the American system. The two systems were founded on different principles and have developed accordingly. More pertinently, the question that should be addressed is whether the UK system is actually fulfilling the constitutional expectations on which it is based. In the field of granting authorisation to government expenditure, where Parliament's effective control and influence is extremely weak, many observers argue that Parliament is not fulfilling these expectations. At the most fundamental level there should be more opportunities for parliamentary debate and consideration of government spending proposals, more opportunities to seek to influence and comment on the government's priorities and greater openness and transparency by government about the choices made and why it has made them. There is also a strong case to be made for greater public discussion and consultation on choices and priorities facing government and for Parliament to be at the forefront of that process. In this report, we look at changes which would provide Parliament with more opportunities to scrutinise and influence spending plans and taxation and thereby obtain greater explanation from government about its proposals and intended outcomes. **Parliament already holds considerable constitutional and procedural powers in this area; the crux of the issue is to ensure that these powers are exercised to achieve a greater interaction and dialogue with government.**

Scrutinising public spending and services

2.7 The role of Parliament is, in some ways, at its most straightforward when it comes to scrutinising past expenditure (and the public services funded by this expenditure) and ensuring that public money is used in the most efficient way possible. Our starting point here is that there should be recognition both within and outside Parliament that financial scrutiny is central to the work of the Commons, since it underpins all other forms of accountability and that parliamentary activity should reflect this. The central principle is that effective scrutiny should improve the way that government operates. By shining a light on waste and inefficiency and following up issues to ensure that problems are resolved, scrutiny should improve the effectiveness of public expenditure and the services that it funds. As we point out, Parliament and its committees, supported by audit bodies such as the NAO, already carry out considerable work in following public money and its effects. Our view is that Parliament could do more systematic and effective financial scrutiny. Crucially, there should be a comprehensive approach to public money in its totality. Nothing should be off limits: Parliament should follow money wherever it goes.

2.8 Improved scrutiny by Parliament would not only give it a stronger influence and impact but would also be to the benefit of government. As Robin Cook argued, when he was Leader of the House of Commons, good scrutiny makes for better government. Why then, given such backing for this virtuous cycle, does it not occur? If Parliament improves its performance and standing by ensuring that government improves itself, and that government is only too happy for this to happen, what stands in the way of improving the system of financial scrutiny? Clearly the political process is not as dispassionate or high minded as such analysis would suggest. The demands on MPs' time, the essentially party political nature of the battle between government and opposition that runs through virtually everything that Parliament does and the unwillingness of any government to readily acknowledge its shortcomings, militate against this taking place. It is these realities that make parliamentary scrutiny both uniquely important – no other body has the constitutional legitimacy for such a role – and also uniquely odd – the search for analysis and improvement is complicated and perhaps even compromised by the stark realities of government and opposition. **Nonetheless, the knowledge that Parliament scrutinises the work of government and requires transparency should help to improve government performance. That is why Parliament should give financial scrutiny as high a priority as possible.**

The role of Parliamentarians

2.9 MPs (and Peers) have many different roles. One of the most important of these, we would argue, is to represent something rather indefinable, namely 'the public interest'. This was a central theme of the report of the Hansard Society Commission on Parliamentary Scrutiny, which argued, 'The task of holding government to account should be central to the parliamentary work of every MP, but in practice it is often defined solely in party political terms. Reforms should seek to enable MPs to balance their party role with their parliamentary role in pursuit of the public interest.'

2.10 Indeed, parliamentarians have already demonstrated that they are able to reconcile the conflicting pressures imposed by their different roles (whether as members of a political party, as parliamentarians or, in the case of MPs, as representatives of their constituents) in environments such as select committees. In the area of financial scrutiny in particular, where there is a strong case for improvement, parliamentarians should build upon the scrutiny systems and culture that currently exist. **Rather than treating scrutiny as solely involving the identification of mistakes, omissions or illegality, the prevailing culture should also move actively into rectification and improvement. These two elements – identifying faults and achieving improvement – should be at the heart of Parliament's scrutiny functions.**

2.11 In section 11, to encourage discussion about the nature of Parliament's scrutiny and accountability functions, we draw attention to two models and guidelines for effective scrutiny processes; one put forward by the Centre for Public Scrutiny and another compiled specifically for this report by PricewaterhouseCoopers.

2.12 In determining what should be done to strengthen parliamentary scrutiny and Parliament's impact on government finance, an important question to ask is whether it is the lack of procedural options that currently constrain MPs or their lack of willingness to engage in such scrutiny? Some of those who gave evidence felt that parliamentarians have traditionally taken little interest in the way that government chooses to spend its money. The problem is particularly acute at the micro-level; understanding of the complex estimates procedure is limited and parliamentarians feel there is little point getting involved in technical details, when there is little chance that their work will have an impact. Discussing the minimal interest taken in debating estimates, Edward Davey MP in his publication, *Making MPs Work for Our Money: Reforming Parliament's Role in Budget Scrutiny* noted, 'Unable to gain any real changes from engaging in budget scrutiny, MPs give up and look elsewhere to exercise influence and power.'[3]

2.13 The problem is accentuated by the tendency to see 'finance' as a category that is separate from other areas and the wider work of government, which often means that MPs do not have the knowledge, interest or inclination to consider such matters. But government finance is not a marginal issue. Despite the impression that it is a complex subject that can be hived off to experts or to the deeply committed, it is in fact fundamental to our political and parliamentary system. One way to engage MPs in financial scrutiny is to create a clear link between policy, finance and service outcomes. MPs are already well acquainted with issues of public service

---

[3] Davey, E (2000) *Making MPs Work for Our Money: Reforming Parliament's Role in Budget Scrutiny,* Centre for Reform, p. 14.

efficiency in their constituencies. But the parliamentary system, and its procedures, do not always make the link between the money raised, the purposes for which the money is spent and the resulting outcomes of that expenditure. **Consequently, a range of different procedures reflect these distinctions. A central challenge for Parliament is to make changes that ensure its scrutiny draws together these apparently disparate elements and achieves more meaningful and effective accountability.**

Supporting financial scrutiny

2.14 In calling for MPs to be more active in carrying out financial scrutiny work there is a danger of thinking of MPs as technicians, which they are not. It is understandable that there may be relatively little knowledge about the technical details of government finance and therefore resources and support are crucial. If MPs are to improve their work in this area they need the fullest support, resources and expert information. The establishment of the Scrutiny Unit has been a significant step forward, and has improved select committee performance in this area. Its value in enhancing the scrutiny work of the Commons depends not only on the quality of its output, but crucially on the interaction with individual select committees and the engagement of individual members of those committees with the information and analysis that it provides. It could also provide support to individual MPs.

2.15 There is a strong case, not only for greater resources for select committees, but also for the provision of a range of suitable skills and expertise within the staff available. The information and support should also be made more accessible to individual members. However, it is not simply a matter of bringing in new staff or even about having adequate resources or support at all. The real question is whether MPs would utilise this extra resource by showing a greater willingness to do more scrutiny work.

The roles of two Houses

2.16 One of Parliament's two Houses, the Lords, has major constitutional restrictions placed upon its powers and functions in financial matters. However, while the Commons has certain financial privileges relating to the authorisation of taxation and public spending, this should not preclude the Lords from taking on more scrutiny functions, particularly by looking in more depth at the effects of government expenditure.

2.17 Greater Lords involvement in scrutiny of expenditure and outcomes would not harm the Commons' financial privilege in the same way that more active involvement in, say, tax raising would. Additionally, the House of Lords could also play a greater role in scrutinising tax administration. Indeed, work already done by the Lords Economic Affairs Committee provides a good model in this area and could be built upon. More broadly, given that reform of the House of Lords is perhaps reaching its endpoint, it is vital that different and innovative ways are considered to ensure that a reformed second chamber plays a central role in seeking and obtaining accountability from government. The role of the House of Lords in financial scrutiny is discussed in section 10.

Parliament and the Public

2.18 In advocating improved parliamentary performance, the direct relevance of Parliament's financial scrutiny work to the public should be borne in mind. As we noted in our interim paper, 'Most people will, understandably, have little interest in mastering the technicalities involved but will expect that a system is in place to ensure that this work happens efficiently on their behalf.' At a time of considerable public disengagement, not to say disenchantment and cynicism with the political process, it is in Parliament's interest to be seen to be making a difference. Parliament will challenge the prevailing cynicism, and perhaps even rise in public esteem, if it is seen to address public concerns and play an active part in helping to deliver improvements to the services that the public receive and which they pay for out of taxation. There is no doubt that the public have strong views about the rate of taxation that they pay and the quality of public services that this funds, even if other indicators of political engagement, such as voting turnout, may show fluctuations or decline.

2.19 There is sometimes a danger of compartmentalising financial issues by taking them out of the wider context and thus detaching them from the day to day concerns of the public. In general, ordinary people are not interested in a category called 'government finance' as such. Therefore, Parliament's work in this area should maintain the link between finance and its impact on the consumers of public services and the people directly or indirectly affected by it. It should also be borne in mind that members of the public often have relevant expertise, knowledge and experience that could enhance the quality of Parliament's work in this field. We discuss further how Parliament can communicate better with the world outside Westminster in section 14.

Achieving change and reform

2.20 The chairman of the PAC, Edward Leigh MP, has argued that:

Departments now have highly developed mechanisms to help them use their resources more productively. Many departments are not using them properly. If they did, they could identify areas of waste or low productivity. Just a small proportion of efficiency gain could save billions of pounds for the tax payer. [4]

While these comments were addressed at government departments, the fundamental question is whether Parliament could also do more in playing a part in achieving these enormous gains. As McEldowney and Lee have noted, 'Overall, Parliament and its agencies do more financial scrutiny than ever before. That scrutiny covers a greater range of public expenditure than ever before.... Parliament and the public have a clearer picture than ever before of the government's overall spending plans.'[5] However, acknowledging that Parliament carries out much good work does not negate the requirement for a better system. McEldowney and Lee also note, 'For at least the last forty years the financial procedures of the House of Commons have seemed ripe for reform...these weaknesses have been only partly tackled in the last forty years.'

2.21 The potential prize from effective reform is enormous, both in financial terms of greater savings and better public services and, crucially, in political terms, in that the political and parliamentary system should deliver what the public want; i.e. the most efficient and effective use of the public's money. Such a search for excellence may smack of idealism and it ultimately lies largely in government's hands to deliver improvements to public services and to the financial efficiency on which they are based. **However, Parliament is uniquely placed to put pressure on government in an effort to ensure that it delivers such changes. It should institute mechanisms to ensure that its pressure is systematically applied to get the best results possible. It is therefore to Parliament that we direct our options for reform and put forward recommendations for change.**

---

[4] PAC press release, 7 April 2005.
[5] McEldowney, J. & Lee, C. (2005) 'Parliament and Public Money' in Giddings, P. (ed.), *The Future of Parliament: Chance or Decay?*, London: Palgrave.

Section 3

Parliamentary Scrutiny of Financial Legislation and Taxation

3.1 It is an article of political faith that very few issues concern the electorate as much as the amount of money taken from them in taxation. In this section, we consider the way that Parliament scrutinises the Budget and the resulting financial legislation. This area of work covers a remarkably broad range of issues, from macro-economic policy (such as the balance of state spending, interest rate policy and economic performance), the efficiency and effectiveness of individual taxes, right through to the difficulties faced by individual taxpayers in filing their returns. Increasingly, with the advent of tax credits and greater interaction between the taxation and social security systems, it also covers issues relating to welfare provision. It is no surprise, therefore, that despite considerable efforts by Parliament in this field, most notably by the Commons Treasury Committee, there is clear scope for reform.

The Budget and the Finance Bill

3.2 Few areas of parliamentary activity attract such a high profile and garner as much media attention as the annual Budget speech (delivered in March or April), during which the Chancellor of the Exchequer sets out the government's economic and financial forecast, and overall plans for spending and taxation. The Budget, and its taxation proposals, are considered in the Commons Chamber during a debate which lasts four to five days and provides Parliament with an opportunity to consider the overall fiscal policy of the government and the totality of the tax and spending settlement. The Budget is also considered in detail by the Commons Treasury Select Committee, which takes oral evidence from the Chancellor of the Exchequer and Treasury officials, as well as from outside experts, and reports back to the House. Frequently, this report back is made after the Finance Bill (which contains the legislative proposals to enact many of the Budget's provisions) has been introduced although in 2005-06 the Committee published its report before the Bill's Second Reading.

3.3 However, in addition to this 'macro-approach' there is scope for additional scrutiny in a number of key areas, in particular for enhanced debate about the government's plans and greater explanation about the choices and priorities that the government has identified. Traditionally, the concept of 'Budget secrecy' has prevented debate about forthcoming proposals to be included in the Budget. This convention has ensured that Parliament has had very little input and influence over the government's thinking. However, over recent years, a Pre-Budget Report (PBR) has been delivered a few months before the Budget (in late November or December). As well as containing updates on the economic and public finance forecast, it has increasingly outlined new policies being considered by government. In fact, the PBR has tended to give a provisional (but fairly accurate) description of many of the measures which will be formally unveiled in the main Budget. Given that the traditional secrecy has been in some senses compromised, there is now more scope and justification for parliamentary input to the process. Currently, the Treasury Committee considers the PBR but a major impediment to effective financial scrutiny relates to the deadlines involved. For example, the Treasury Committee has to rush through consideration of the PBR before Christmas. In fact, there are another three months before the Budget is unveiled and some of this time could be used for committee inquiries or full debates on the details of what has been announced. As with many aspects of parliamentary scrutiny, there is a greater chance of influencing the government before a policy (or legislative proposal) is announced and the formal process set in motion. **Therefore, the period between the Budget and the PBR presents opportunities for parliamentary committees to take expert and public evidence on the outline of the government's plans and to make a case for priorities it wishes government to consider. There should be more opportunities to debate and question government proposals. At the very least it should ensure that government makes the case and provides full information, on the initiatives that it plans to bring forward.** There would need to be an agreed cut off point by which time Parliament should make its input, giving the government sufficient time to respond. Given that the PBR contains an outline of both the intended direction of macro-economic policy as well as some indication of provisional tax measures, there is considerable scope and time for parliamentary input and debate on these different and crucial elements of the Budget process.

Timing of the Budget

3.4 There is also the question of the timing of the Budget itself, which is presented to Parliament shortly before the Easter parliamentary recess, leaving little opportunity for parliamentary debate (in 2006 the Budget was presented to Parliament on 22 March, just a week before the parliamentary recess). The Organisation for Economic Co-operation and Development (OECD) has issued guidelines on Budget transparency, which state that:

The government's draft budget should be submitted to Parliament far enough in advance to allow Parliament to review it properly. In no case should this be less than three months prior to the start of the fiscal year....The Budget is the government's key policy document. It should be comprehensive, encompassing all government revenue and expenditure, so that the necessary trade-offs between different policy options can be assessed. [6]

While it could be argued that the PBR enables Parliament to consider some of the issues which will be raised in the Budget, in reality, the parliamentary process following the PBR does not allow for, or indeed encourage, close scrutiny or input into the comprehensive picture of government spending and taxation, and policy priorities.

3.5 There is also the question of the amount of notice traditionally given by the Chancellor of the dates of the PBR and Budget. It has been put to us that these are typically too short for relevant organisations to prepare. **There is, therefore, an argument that the dates for such important statements should be set well in advance or perhaps even be on a fixed date.**

Scrutiny of the Finance Bill

3.6 At the other end of the Budget process comes the Finance Bill, which enables many of the Budget provisions to be enacted. Although the Budget and Finance Bill are inextricably linked, in many ways they need to be recognised as two separate entities. The focus of the Budget (and also, in essence, the PBR) is on the macro-economic position. These 'macro' issues tend to dominate the broader parliamentary debate which leaves the detailed scrutiny of tax changes to the committee stage of the Finance Bill. The Finance Bill, containing many of the government's income raising proposals and detailed taxation changes, is introduced a few weeks after the Budget. The Second Reading of the Bill, which usually lasts a full day, allows MPs to consider the government's taxation system and priorities. Unlike the case with most legislation, the more controversial clauses are considered by a Committee of the Whole House for two to three days, before the rest of the Bill is considered clause by clause in Standing Committee.[7] The committee is usually made up of 30 to 40 members – double the membership used for most legislation. It should also be noted that the Treasury is guaranteed parliamentary time for its annual Finance Bill, in contrast with other departments which have to compete for space. This 'exceptionalism' applies in other respects, most particularly in that many

---

[6] OECD, (May 2001) OECD *Best Practices for Budget Transparency*, p. 4.
[7] The motion selecting the clauses to be discussed on the floor of the House is put forward by the government, though in practice the opposition determines the content.

of the recent changes to the legislative process, such a pre-legislative scrutiny, have not extended to the Finance Bill. This is just one of the reasons why there is significant scope to improve parliamentary scrutiny of taxation issues.

3.7 In theory, the committee stage of the Finance Bill allows Parliament an opportunity to scrutinise and improve the quality of the legislation. However, in practice, as with much legislation, the debate is generally divided along party lines, and the government's majority in the committee ensures that its proposals are passed in the form that it wishes. It has been argued that the government may in fact be more determined to ensure that the Bill is passed with few changes, given its impact on government finances and activity. In addition, the defects that many commentators have identified with the legislative process – notably haphazard scrutiny resulting in key clauses being undebated – are particularly evident. However, perhaps the greatest challenge to effective scrutiny is the increasingly complex and lengthy nature of the Bill itself, which runs to many hundreds of pages. Edward Davey MP described the defects in the scrutiny of the Finance Bill:

There are a number of serious structural and technical problems with the Finance Bill procedure. These... prevent the process from having a more positive effect on the resulting tax legislation. The most frustrating part of the Finance Bill process is that the sub-standard tax legislation it produces could be avoided at no political cost or loss of Executive control. .... This arises from the fact that the vast bulk of every Finance Bill is made up of technical changes that are not politically contentious. However, partly because of time constraints and partly because of the endemic partisan nature of Standing Committees, even non-contentious changes proposed by opposition MPs have come to be seen as political attacks which must be repelled. [8]

In short, given the length of the Bill, its technical complexities, the tight control of government and the inevitable disparity in the expertise of the MPs considering it, measures can be passed without genuine scrutiny of the implications of the provisions.

3.8 The question of improving scrutiny of the Finance Bill should be seen in the wider context of the innovations that have improved legislative scrutiny in recent years, most notably pre-legislative scrutiny and the consideration of draft bills by committees. Financial legislation has generally not benefited from these changes and there is a strong case that financial legislation should be treated the same as other legislation. As discussed, many of the reasons for treating financial legislation differently (most notably, budget secrecy) have disappeared, particularly with the introduction of the PBR.

---

[8] Davey, E (ibid) p. 21.

3.9 Currently, only a few clauses of the Budget are released beforehand. In fact, much more of the Finance Bill, if not its entirety, should be published in draft so that practitioners and interested parties can look at it and feed into the committee considering it in detail. Pre-legislative scrutiny can be carried out in a number of ways. The most commonly used method is consideration of draft bills by the relevant departmental select committee. The Treasury Committee, as has been noted, already covers an enormous area of work and may simply not have sufficient time and capacity to add extra functions. **An ad hoc committee in the Commons could be constituted to undertake such pre-legislative scrutiny.**

Scrutiny of Taxation and Tax Administration

3.10 There are a number of separate issues relating to the detailed scrutiny of taxation. There is scrutiny of the overall revenue settlement and the way that the total is raised through individual taxes and duties. In addition, there are the distinct areas of scrutiny of the effectiveness and impact of individual taxes, in terms of their impact on individuals, family policy or business, for example. Another separate but crucially important area of work is the consideration of the way that the tax system is administered and how individuals and companies relate to, and are affected by, tax administration.

3.11 Given the range of different issues that it contains, there have been calls, so far without success, for the Finance Bill to be split into two major annual bills: one containing changes to tax legislation and a separate one concerning tax administration. Some of the detailed scrutiny of tax legislation and financial proposals is already undertaken by the Commons Treasury Committee, which has an overriding remit in this area, but given the constraints on its time, issues such as tax legislation and administration are given a relatively low priority. Some extra work in this area has recently been undertaken by the House of Lords Economic Affairs committee but it seems clear that much more work on this subject could be carried out, as one former member of the Treasury Committee, David Laws MP, explained:

Having served on the Treasury Committee, I am not convinced that it has been able in the past to give enough attention to specific tax measures, as opposed to the macro-economic impact of budgets. Therefore, it has not been able to inform the debates that we have in this place, especially by taking evidence from outside bodies. For that reason, I welcome the fact that the House of Lords Committee has again prepared a report on the Finance Bill and I hope that we shall be able to learn from some of its assessments, often made by people with much expertise in the area who have considered the issues in a non-party political and non-partisan way.[9]

---

[9] House of Commons Hansard, 6 July 2004, col. 778.

A leading article in *The Guardian* was particularly trenchant in its criticism of the Treasury Committee, describing it as 'one of Parliament's more toothless watchdogs; it has little in the way of meaningful bite'.[10]

3.12 We outline a number of alternative options that could ensure more effective scrutiny by parliamentary committees of tax law and administration. (Obviously it would not be suitable for all these options to be introduced at the same time: they represent alternatives that would lead to the same end.)

- The formation of a **separate Tax Committee in the House of Commons,** has been recommended by George Cunningham, a former MP and former member of the Procedure Committee, in evidence to this inquiry. He noted:

    The [Committee Stage] on Finance Bills is not a suitable vehicle for examining taxation. There are many aspects of tax policy and tax administration that would benefit from the kind of leisurely study that a select committee can give. Are 10 per cent, 22 per cent and 40 per cent the best figures for income tax? Does it make sense to have an Inheritance Tax regime which is a far greater burden on the modestly well off as against the very well off? There are hundreds of other aspects of tax law and practice which would benefit from the type of studies that only a select committee can do. The Treasury Committee just does not have time to do this.

- **The formation of a Tax Administration Committee, which would look at the development of tax law and the way that such law is implemented and administered.** This might take the form of a Commons committee. Another possibility would be the formation of a Joint Committee of both Houses assuming that the principle of the financial precedence of the Commons is safeguarded and that its remit was confined to tax administration. There is already one relevant committee, the existing Tax Law Rewrite Committee (TLRWC), which looks specifically at bills coming out of the Tax Law Rewrite process.[11] A new committee of this type could subsume the work of the TLRWC.

- Looking at external options to strengthen parliamentary scrutiny, another option would be the **establishment of a Tax Law Commission**, which would take an overview of the effectiveness of tax legislation and make proposals for change. Alternatively **the Law Commission's powers could be extended to cover tax legislation.** Such bodies could provide an extra mechanism to look in detail at the operation and effectiveness of tax law, take evidence from experts and the public and provide reports that would strengthen parliamentary scrutiny in this area.

---

[10] *The Guardian*, 24 May 2006.
[11] The Tax Law Rewrite Committee has seven members from each House and met for the first time in January 2001 with a remit to modernise tax legislation without altering its substance.

The formation of an HMRC Committee

3.13 One option, in addition to those outlined above, would be for a separate select committee to cover the areas covered by Her Majesty's Revenue and Customs (HMRC). In 2005, HMRC was created as a new department through the merger of the Inland Revenue and Her Majesty's Customs and Excise. HMRC is responsible for the collection of direct taxes (such as income tax and corporation tax), indirect taxes (such as value added tax) and some import controls, and also for national insurance contributions. The area of tax administration and revenue collection is, in itself, a clear contender for improved scrutiny and oversight. Two recent reports indicated the scope of the issues involved. The PAC highlighted the fact that mistakes in tax returns are costing the Exchequer an estimated £2.8 billion[12] Additionally, the HMRC estimated that about £10 billion is being lost to tax avoidance schemes and announced that it was setting up a special unit to investigate such schemes.[13] Conversely, it is safe to assume that mistakes in tax administration may also be adding unwarranted costs to individual taxpayers.

3.14 Critically, in recent years substantial areas of work, which were previously the domain of the Department of Social Security/Work and Pensions, have been transferred to the ministerial control of the Treasury, including the large and complex national insurance system. Child benefit, with its vast caseload, has also been added. Most significantly, the advent of a system of tax credits to direct support to families in work and also encompassing other social policy initiatives, has opened up new areas of work for the HMRC. This issue has particular resonance given that the system has been subject to serious administrative difficulties. In 2006, for example, the Treasury confirmed that overpayments of tax credits for 2004/05 totalled £1.8 billion compared to £2.2 billion for the previous year.[14]

3.15 As mentioned, the Treasury Committee covers a very broad range of work, including macro-economic issues such as interest rate policy and Pre- and Main Budget inquiries as well as issues such as financial services. Currently, a sub-committee of the Treasury Committee scrutinises issues relating to HMRC. Because of the enormous scope of its overall remit, it is clear that the Treasury Committee is overstretched. As a result its ability to scrutinise effectively all the areas it has to cover is compromised. The scope and importance of this work warrants closer and more detailed scrutiny. Furthermore, a separate HMRC

---

[12] Public Accounts Committee (2005-06) *Filing of Income Tax Self Assessment Returns*, HC 681.
[13] See BBC News Online, 2 March 2006 citing *The Money Programme*, BBC Television.
[14] HM Treasury, Written Ministerial Statement, 5 June 2006.

committee would be likely to attract significant interest, both from the media and public, and also most likely within Parliament too. **We recommend that a separate HMRC committee should be established, possibly by converting the existing Treasury Sub-Committee on the HMRC into a separate committee to provide closer scrutiny of the many areas covered by the HMRC.**

Section 4

Parliamentary Scrutiny of Expenditure Plans

4.1 There are a number of formal and informal mechanisms for parliamentary involvement in authorising and scrutinising government spending plans. Financial scrutiny in this area can occur at the macro level – involving scrutiny of government spending priorities and how public money should be split between different government departments. It can also take place at the micro-level and involves detailed analysis of spending plans and allocations within departments. The evidence gathered by this inquiry suggests that Parliament has traditionally been more active in debating and scrutinising fundraising and taxation rather than detailed plans for government expenditure. This is partly due to the lack of opportunities for parliamentarians to have an impact on the setting of government spending priorities, as a result of which the formal mechanisms for parliamentary input are viewed as exercises in 'box ticking'.

4.2 Overall our review points to three areas in which reform is required. Firstly, **more opportunities for the House of Commons to be involved in the scrutiny of government spending** are needed, particularly at an early stage in the spending review process. Secondly, **the resources of the Scrutiny Unit and the NAO should be more extensively utilised** by Commons committees to scrutinise government spending plans, particularly through consideration of departmental annual reports (DARs, often referred to as departmental reports). Thirdly, **the scrutiny work carried out by committees needs to be linked to the formal processes for financial scrutiny and authorisation,** to ensure that their reports receive the full attention of the House, and inform its work.

The Estimates Process

4.3 The supply process, through which the government seeks Parliament's approval for its annual spending plans, currently provides the main formal avenue for parliamentary scrutiny. Spending requests from government are put to Parliament in the form of supply estimates, which detail the resources required for the individual programmes of government departments. The bulk of requests are put to Parliament in April or May in the main estimates shortly after the Budget Statement, though in-year changes to departmental budgets are also made through the introduction of supplementary or revised estimates.

4.4 MPs have an opportunity to scrutinise and debate estimates on the floor of the House on three 'estimate days' in each parliamentary session. Discussion on these days focuses on select committee reports linked to the estimates that are selected by the House of Commons Liaison Committee. Estimates themselves are, to a large extent, voted on and approved in bulk at the end of a parliamentary sitting with little or no debate. On the estimates day in December 2004, for example, the House of Commons authorised over £320 billion of government expenditure following a two-hour debate, which primarily focused on government IT projects. This is not to say that the debates on estimate days are not valuable: they can provide an opportunity for Parliament to make the link between finance and government policy. However, given the short amount of time provided for debating estimates, it is essential that Parliament uses other opportunities to authorise and scrutinise government expenditure. It is for this reason that we also look at DARs and parliamentary input into spending reviews.

4.5 Explanatory memoranda on estimates are also sent to the relevant departmental select committees, which have an opportunity to scrutinise individual estimates before they are debated. Departments are asked (though not required) by the Treasury to provide committees with a final draft of the resource estimate to the committee as soon as they are signed off. The government argues that 'for many departments the tight timetable for producing supplementary estimates means that they are completed only very shortly before they are printed and published versions presented to Parliament'.[15]

4.6 The government gains the legal authority to spend funds set out in estimates through the passage of two Appropriation Acts and one Consolidated Fund Act a year. It is assumed that the measures in the Bills have already been debated on estimate days, even though, as already noted, little time is spent debating specific estimates. They are therefore passed without debate at any of the formal stages.[16]

4.7 The majority of people who gave evidence to this inquiry were of the view that the supply process as it currently operates, while being very complex, is little more than a 'rubber stamp'. Sir Nicholas Winterton MP stated: 'Estimate Day debates are extremely low-key, with amendments and divisions almost unknown. Also debates have tended to focus on policy, rather than expenditure and were a somewhat artificial peg on which to hang a debate on a committee report on a more general subject.' While it is procedurally possible for an MP to table a motion to reduce an

---

[15] Liaison Committee (2005-06) *The Government Reply to the Annual Report for 2004*, HC 855.
[16] Given the principle of Commons precedence on financial matters, the House of Lords has no power to block or amend Commons' approval of supply: only their formal approval is required before the Bills receive Royal Assent.

estimate, or for an estimate to be rejected by a vote in the Commons, in practice this never happens. As the Hansard Society's Commission on Parliamentary Scrutiny noted: 'Parliament has one real sanction: to reject the government's spending proposals. With the majority of MPs being members of the governing party, they are most unlikely to take this "nuclear option". The effects of a lack of subtlety and real options means that government can safely take Parliament for granted.'

4.8 In 1999 the Commons Procedure Committee made proposals to give Parliament a more influential role in the supply process, including by being able to transfer totals between budget heads for a particular department. It argued:

The principle of the financial initiative of the Crown rightly precludes motions recommending increases to the Estimates themselves. However, we consider that when motions are directed to future plans, motions recommending that 'in the opinion of the House' increases in expenditure or transfers between certain budgets are desirable and should be permissible.[17]

However, the proposals were rejected by the Treasury on the grounds that it would 'undermine the financial initiative of the crown.'[18] Since 1999 several procedural changes described by the Procedure Committee as 'useful, but minor' have been introduced.[19] They include the introduction of two Appropriation Acts and greater time for select committees to scrutinise estimates. However, the general consensus is that the changes have done little to strengthen Parliament's ability to scrutinise government spending or have a more meaningful say in how public money is spent.

4.9 Many contributors to this inquiry felt that there was little to be gained from simply concentrating on the supply process, which essentially involves approving spending plans that have already been made. In this context, it is understandable that there is little appetite within Parliament for detailed debate and involvement, if they know that it is already too late to have any genuine impact. **Where reform is needed is at an earlier stage in the process, so that Parliament could have a more active role in determining what the government's spending priorities should be. Greater involvement in the spending review and estimates processes and more systematic analysis of DARs by select committees would be more effective ways of strengthening Parliament's scrutiny of spending.** As we argued in section 3.3, the tradition of Budget secrecy and the inhibitions that it has placed on parliamentary scrutiny do not apply to the same extent as they have before.

---

[17] Procedure Committee (1998-1999) *The Procedure for Debate on the Government's Expenditure Plans*, HC 295.
[18] Procedure Committee (1999-2000) *Government Response to the Sixth Report of the Session 1998-1999: Procedure for Debate on the Government's Expenditure Plans*, HC 388.
[19] PAC (2003-04) *Estimates and Appropriation Procedure*, HC 393.

4.10 Nevertheless, is there a way of making the supply process more accessible to parliamentarians and the public and at the same time offer Parliament a more active role in scrutinising and authorising governing spending plans? Certainly, the work already done by committees to scrutinise estimates, supported by the Scrutiny Unit, should be welcomed, and further built upon. We reiterate the recommendation recently made by the Liaison Committee that **government departments should be required to present draft estimates, alongside explanatory memorandum, at the earliest practicable date.**[20] However, given the complexity of the material being considered they point to the need for further resources to support this work (see Section 13 for a further discussion of the Scrutiny Unit and resources to support the work of parliamentarians).

Spending Reviews

4.11 The estimates presented to Parliament are based on government spending reviews, which set firm three-year plans for departmental expenditure. In 1997 the incoming Labour government announced the first Comprehensive Spending Review (CSR). The review professed to take a 'root and branch' look at spending across departments to ensure that public money was spent in line with the government's priorities and included an analysis of whether spending was in the public interest, whether current expenditure was the best way of meeting government objectives, and whether there was scope for improved efficiency and effectiveness. The results of the CSR were published in the White Paper *Modern Public Services for Britain: Investing in Reform, Comprehensive Spending Review: New Public Spending Plans 1999-2002*. The paper set out firm expenditure allocations between departments for the next three years, as well as the long-term government priorities, against which government spending plans could be measured. The review also introduced Public Service Agreements (PSAs), which set performance targets for government departments. Between 1998 and 2004, spending reviews setting out firm three year expenditure plans took place every two years, with the most recent in 2004 setting out plans for the period of 2005-08. Unlike the 1998 review, however, these have not sought to examine government spending from a zero base. The next CSR, which will operate from a zero base, is due to take place in 2007.

4.12 The evidence received by this inquiry suggests that spending reviews (and in particular the forthcoming CSR) with their summaries of departmental

---

[20] Liaison Committee (2005-06) *The Government Reply to the Annual Report for 2004*, HC 855.

objectives, firm expenditure plans for forthcoming years and analysis of cross departmental issues, provide the ideal opportunity for Parliament to scrutinise government spending plans at both the macro and the micro level. However, the timetable for the reviews, which are generally published in July, shortly before the long summer recess, limits the opportunity for detailed parliamentary scrutiny, particularly by select committees. Instead most of the scrutiny takes place within the main chamber and there is little opportunity for committees to conduct a thorough analysis of budget allocations between and within departments.

4.13 Several participants in our seminar felt that a major step forward would be for Parliament to be more fully involved in the process leading up to the announcement of the outcome of the CSR expected in the summer of 2007. Parliament should subject the interim report on the CSR to detailed scrutiny. There is also a question of whether there should be a more formal role for Parliament in the spending review process, as is the case in Scotland (see Box A). While spending priorities may be debated in Parliament, there is no formal mechanism for concerns or priorities identified by parliamentarians to be fed back to the government. The interim report on the CSR, due to be published by the Government in mid-2006, will provide material for committees to consider and stimulate a wider debate within Parliament. The concerns could then be fed back to government and influence how it sets its priorities. Moreover the government is more likely to accept (and less likely to see as an issue of confidence) changes that are proposed early on in the agenda setting process.[21]

4.14 Therefore at one level it requires a greater willingness by the government to open up the CSR process to scrutiny and input by Parliament. **This includes presenting the interim report sufficiently early in the parliamentary calendar for committees to be able to carry out thorough scrutiny and to feed these comments to the government. At the same time it requires greater commitment from Parliament to rise to the challenge and make full use of the material in the interim report to scrutinise and debate government spending priorities.**

---

[21] This is certainly the case with pre-legislative scrutiny: recommendations by parliamentary committees on draft legislation have more of an impact as conceding to change at this stage is seen as less of a direct challenge. For further information see Brazier, A (2004) *Pre-legislative scrutiny: Issues in Law Making Paper 5,* Hansard Society: London.

BOX A: The Scottish Parliament and the Budget[22]

The Scottish Parliament, and in particular its committees, has an active role in setting the Executive's spending priorities. Its involvement takes place through a three step process in spending review years. A more simplified process of consultation takes place in non-spending review years.[23]

Stage One: April – June Year 1: In April, the Executive submits a provisional expenditure plan called the annual evaluation report to Parliament for each year of the spending review period. The document is intended to provide Parliament with an opportunity to take a strategic look at the budget early in the process and to make recommendations in consultation with the public and stakeholders. The Finance Committee oversees the consultation process within Parliament. All subject committees report to the Finance Committee on the relationship between expenditure plans and policy priorities in their relevant spending area, in consultation with external bodies. The Finance Committee produces a report, which is presented to and debated in Parliament in June. The executive then produces a draft budget in light of the report and the debate within Parliament.

Stage Two: September – December Year 1: In September, the Executive produces its draft budget, containing firm spending plans for the following financial year. Once again, parliamentary scrutiny is coordinated by the Finance Committee, which consults with other committees on the particular parts of the budget which are relevant to them, and assesses the extent to which the Executive has taken on board comments made in Stage One. The Finance Committee has the option of putting forward an alternative budget with the proviso that this must keep within the overall spending limit set by the Executive's draft budget. The Finance Committee produces a report by early December, which is then debated in a plenary session. Individual Members may seek to propose amendments to the Executive's expenditure proposals by tabling amendments to the Finance Committee motion.

---

[22] This section draws on evidence submitted by the Scottish Parliament to the inquiry.
[23] In these years only Stages One and Two take place.

> **Stage Three: January – February Year 2:** In January, the Executive presents Parliament with its annual budget Bill, providing parliamentary authority for spending in the following financial year. The Bill is given a speedier passage through Parliament than other bills, and only members of the Executive may move amendments to the Bill. Parliament has a vote to accept or reject the Bill.
>
> Despite the swift passage of the budget Bill, and the inability of ordinary Members to introduce amendments to the Bill, the three-stage process gives Parliament a greater stake in the budgetary process. While this process does not guarantee that the proposals are included in the subsequent budget Bill, they do allow Parliament to thoroughly scrutinise and debate government spending plans and provides a much greater opportunity to influence the Bill early in the process.

Departmental Annual Reports

4.15 The information contained in DARs provides Parliament with an opportunity to conduct detailed scrutiny of government spending plans, at a macro and micro level. The reports, which are published by individual government departments between March and May each year, set out departmental aims, objectives and principal activities, expenditure plans (including firm plans for the following year and estimates of spending in future years) and achievements (including PSA targets). Since they were first published in 1991, consideration of the reports has taken place almost exclusively in select committees. The ability of committees to scrutinise expenditure related issues arising from such reports has been bolstered by the work of the Scrutiny Unit. Since June 2005 the Unit has considered 21 DARs on behalf of departmental select committees. A number of committees have also undertaken detailed reviews of their department's resource accounts.[24]

4.16 Scrutiny of departmental reports has enabled committees to conduct a comprehensive analysis of government spending priorities, both within and across departments. For example, the recent report of the Education and Skills Committee

---

[24] For example the Northern Ireland Affairs Committee examined all Northern Ireland departments' resource accounts in 2004.

on *Public Expenditure on Education and Skills* contained analysis and recommendations on government spending on education.[25]

4.17 Despite progress in this area there are no formal mechanisms for the scrutiny work of select committees to be fed into the wider work of Parliament or to government. **One option for reform is to introduce a formal requirement that the relevant departmental select committee consider the DAR and be asked to approve it. If a committee expresses its concerns about a DAR through publication of a report, a debate could then take place in Westminster Hall or in the Main Chamber (determined by the Liaison Committee). An alternative would be for the Liaison Committee to publish a report on the totality of departmental reports, on which a debate could then take place.** This would bring the subject of departmental spending into the wider domain of the Commons and enable MPs to debate not only the details of specific spending programmes of government departments (departmental micro level), but also their overall direction and spending priorities.

4.18 Concerns have been expressed over the ability of committees to cope with this extra work load: certainly even with the additional support provided by the Scrutiny Unit the many demands upon committees can limit their capacity to carry out effective detailed financial scrutiny. The Hansard Society's Scrutiny Commission recommended the establishment of a Finance and Audit Sub-Committee for each departmental select committee to consider finance and audit by subject area and focus on plans, estimates and outturn. **We recommend that Finance and Audit Sub-Committees should be piloted in a number of select committees.** In the first instance, such sub committees should be piloted to assess whether they would attract sufficient interest from MPs and to judge whether this model succeeds in strengthening the financial work of select committees. The select committees which would benefit from this approach include those with large and/or complicated expenditure issues such as Defence, Work and Pensions and Health. There is an argument that such a sub-committee might compartmentalise financial issues, thus detaching them from the mainstream of the committee's work. On the contrary, the rationale of this proposal is that financial scrutiny requires a distinct forum and specific high priority. It would be essential that a Finance and Audit Sub-Committee would feed its work into the main committee and would be charged with undertaking its work on behalf of the main committee. Crucially, the sub-committee's membership (with support from the Scrutiny Unit as well as designated staff) would develop particular expertise in

---

[25] Education and Skills Committee (2005-06) *Public Expenditure on Education and Skills*, HC 479.

this subject. The proposal for a Finance and Audit Sub-Committee is further considered in section 5.20.

The balance between the legislature and the executive

4.19 Internationally, there is considerable variation in the role that legislatures have in the budgetary process. This role is determined partly by constitutional constraints, and partly by the political context within which they operate.[26] Broadly speaking legislatures fall into three main categories:[27]

- Legislatures that have the capacity to amend or reject executive spending proposals and the capacity to formulate an alternative budget of their own. The United States Congress falls into this category: there are no constitutional limits on the budgetary powers of Congress, which can spend over eight months debating the budget.

- Legislatures with influence over spending proposals, which can amend or reject spending proposals but cannot formulate or substitute them with their own. According to the IMF 63 per cent of legislatures make minor adjustments, including Scandinavian countries, such as Sweden and Finland.

- Legislatures that cannot (realistically) amend or reject spending proposals or are barred from substituting a budget of their own. They are confined to assenting to spending proposals as they are put to them. The United Kingdom Parliament falls into this category, along with other countries such as Canada and Australia with legislatures based on the Westminster model. The last time a request for money was voted down by the UK Parliament was in 1919.

4.20 Even if the UK does not move to the US model, the question remains how reforms could be introduced to give Parliament greater influence – rather than control – over the budget. As the World Bank Institute notes, effective legislative participation in the budget process is vital as it 'establishes checks and balances that are crucial for transparent and accountable government and ensuring the efficient delivery of public services...As the representative institutions of the people it falls down to national legislatures to ensure that the budget optimally matches a nation's need with available resources'.[28] Crucially, an ability to have a greater impact on the budget can also have an impact on the willingness of MPs to take part in the debate. One of the reasons why

---

[26] For further analysis of the factors that determine the role of the legislature, see Lienert, I. (2005) *Who Controls the Budget: The Legislature or the Executive?* International Monetary Fund.
[27] The distinction was made in a World Bank Institute paper on gender budgeting. See Wehner, J. & Byanyima, W., *Parliament, the Budget and Gender,* World Bank Institute: Washington DC.
[28] Wehner, J. & Byanyima, W., *(ibid)*, p. 9.

there is little enthusiasm for detailed scrutiny of spending plans within Parliament is the negligible impact they have on the policy making process. **Reform of the system of financial scrutiny should not aim to take control over spending out of the hands of the executive. Rather it should aim to open the system up to improved parliamentary scrutiny and greater parliamentary input, influence and public comment.**

Box B: International comparison of budgetary powers

The striking variation in the impact that national legislatures have on the budgetary process is illustrated in the figure below. Based on the index of the budgetary powers of national legislatures drawn up by the International Monetary Fund (IMF), it measures: whether the legislature approves an annual budget strategy; the extent of its powers to amend draft budgets; the time for discussion of the annual budget within the legislature; the technical support received for scrutinising the budget and the government's ability to modify the budget once it has been approved.[29] It is not an indication of the overall system of financial scrutiny in place in the legislature. Only the United States has the highest possible score of 10. The United Kingdom on the other hand scores 1, with only one country (New Zealand), scoring zero.

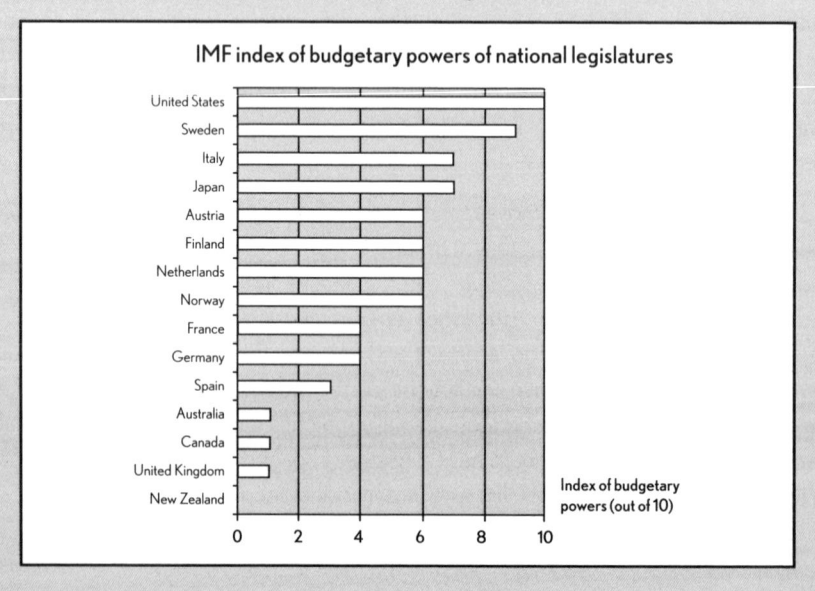

IMF index of budgetary powers of national legislatures

Country	Index of budgetary powers (out of 10)
United States	10
Sweden	9
Italy	7
Japan	7
Austria	6
Finland	6
Netherlands	6
Norway	6
France	5
Germany	5
Spain	3
Australia	1
Canada	1
United Kingdom	1
New Zealand	0

---

[29] See Lienert, I. (2005), ibid, 'Table 2: Indices for the Legislature's Budget Authority in 28 countries'.

Section 5

Parliamentary Scrutiny of Government Expenditure

5.1 Parliamentary scrutiny of government expenditure, after the money has been spent, is widely regarded as the stronger aspect of its scrutiny of government finance, certainly when compared to the effectiveness of authorisation of future expenditure. In this section we look at developments in this area and, in particular, consider ways in which Parliament could more effectively scrutinise public expenditure and the delivery of public services. We focus on the work of the National Audit Office (NAO) and the Public Accounts Committee (PAC), and the role of select committees and consider the subject of 'joined-up' work in this area. In following sections we consider the specific role of the Audit Commission and look at developments in the devolved institutions.

The work of the National Audit Office and the Public Accounts Committee

5.2 In our discussion paper, we outlined the work of the NAO, the independent parliamentary body headed by the Comptroller and Auditor General (C&AG). The C&AG, with the NAO's support, has a statutory responsibility to audit the financial statements of all central government departments, agencies and other public bodies, and to report the results of his examinations to Parliament. In 2004-05 the NAO audited over 570 accounts covering some £800 billion of revenue and expenditure (although the actual numbers of accounts audited varies from year to year).

5.3 The primary objective of the NAO's financial audit is to provide independent assurance, information and advice to Parliament on the proper accounting for and use of public resources. The other main function of the NAO is to provide independent reports to Parliament on the economy, efficiency and effectiveness with which government departments and other bodies use their resources. These value for money reports take a focused look at how specific government programmes, projects and activities have been implemented. Two years ago, in response to demands from Parliament to increase scrutiny of public spending programmes, the C&AG increased the number of value for money reports produced by the NAO from 50 to 60 a year. Most, but not all, of the C&AG's reports to Parliament are considered by the PAC.

5.4 In addition to its direct relationship with the PAC, the NAO also provides support to departmental select committees both by seconding staff and by providing oral and written evidence. This has included the production of seven briefing papers for the Environmental Audit Committee over the past two years. The Public Accounts Commission has recently made extra resources available to the NAO to contribute to the work of other select committees, which has included oral or written briefings to the Treasury, Transport, Public Administration and Work & Pensions Committees. This work could also provide opportunities for committees to take evidence on NAO reports, which have not been before the PAC.

Making a difference: the impact of the PAC

5.5 The PAC takes oral evidence in public (with briefings produced by the NAO) from the departmental permanent secretaries or agency chief executives who, as accounting officers, have a direct and personal responsibility for their organisation's expenditure, and other relevant witnesses such as senior executives from private sector contractors. The PAC considers the evidence and publishes its own report with recommendations. With the backing of the NAO and its staff of over 800, the PAC produces approximately 50 reports a year, far more than other select committees. According to the NAO, the government responds to about 1,000 recommendations from the PAC in an average Parliament, and accepts about 95 per cent of them. In 2004, the NAO estimated that by following its recommendations, the Government had secured savings for the taxpayer of £515 million. The NAO has a target of saving £8 for every £1 that it spends, which it exceeded, once again, in 2004. In addition, the deterrent effect of the work of the NAO and PAC has a definite, but less quantifiable, impact in promoting efficiency and safeguarding public funds.

5.6 Despite the figures for savings and the importance of the work of both the NAO and PAC, the system is not without its critics. These criticisms include, for example, that the enormous scope of government means that even with the resources of the NAO, the PAC has to be selective in what it considers and can only take a limited look at government expenditure. The question has been raised whether the overarching nature of the PAC's remit means that it has to cover such an enormous range of subjects that it is unable to go into enough depth on each one (in contrast to some inquiries undertaken on similar subjects by the departmental select committees). Furthermore, there is the perception that, given the extremely broad nature of the Committee's work, individual members of the PAC are simply unable to develop sufficient expertise in all the areas that they are expected to cover and that this limits the effectiveness of the Committee.

5.7 Most pertinently, one issue that has been frequently raised, for example by David Walker, (Editor, Public Magazine, *The Guardian*) is whether the work of the NAO/PAC is followed up as effectively as it might be. The NAO's evidence to this inquiry stated that 95 per cent of the PAC's recommendations are accepted by the government, and that reviews of accepted recommendations have shown that in 99 per cent of cases action had been taken.[30] Even so, there is suspicion that some recommendations gather dust and are not followed by any action. A 2005 PAC report, *Achieving Value for Money in the Delivery of Public Services*, suggested that while there had been progress on following up recommendations from most reports, with others little action has been taken.[31] Such action is not simply a matter for the Treasury, despite its role in formally replying to the PAC. In most cases, it is up to individual government departments to take the action required. The Government certainly gives a high priority to the work of the PAC, as it acknowledged in its reply to the PAC's 2005 report:

The Government takes the Committee's recommendations seriously as the fruit of the accountability process. The best proof of this is that, as the report acknowledges, the great majority of the Committee's recommendations have been acted upon. The Committee has thus helped the Government to secure financial savings, raise the standards of public services and improve the quality of delivery. [32]

5.8 There is, of course, potentially a significant difference between the implications of the Government position (i.e. that the PAC has an almost universally successful impact on government) and what actually happens in practice. As the Hansard Society Commission on Parliamentary Scrutiny pointed out, sometimes the action taken by government in response to PAC reports and those of other select committees can be quite limited in practice, if it even happens at all. Edward Davey MP has also questioned the extent and nature of the follow-up work undertaken:

I have a major concern that many good ideas and much hard work is effectively lost, because of the lack of systematic follow-up. Although public policy debates are now peppered with buzz words such as 'evidence-based policy', 'best-practice' and 'best value', there is a shocking lack of systematic learning ...There remains a case for a more strategic follow-up, to ensure that lessons have been learnt, that the Executive has answered PAC criticisms fully and that ministers have engaged in the issues raised, and not simply left ex post scrutiny issues to the civil servants. [33]

---

[30] The NAO undertakes work to follow up how effectively departments have implemented the recommendations of the PAC; see the NAO's Annual Report 2005 (p. 22) on *Managing Attendance in the Department of Work and Pensions* and details provided in its Corporate Plan 2006-07 to 2008-09 (p. 25).

[31] PAC (2005-06) *Achieving Value for Money in the Delivery of Public Services*, HC 742.

[32] Treasury Minute, February 2006, Cm 6743.

[33] Davey, E. (ibid) p. 46.

5.9 The real test of the influence of the PAC is not simply whether its recommendations are accepted by government but whether they are in fact implemented, effectively and in full, and, most importantly, whether they make a positive difference to financial efficiency and quality of service. For this reason, our central recommendations in this area concern more systematic follow-up of the work of the NAO and PAC, an issue further discussed later in this section.

Innovation and improvement

5.10 The fundamental question is whether Parliament's scrutiny work promotes better and more efficient government? Since the issue of government efficiency was brought into the political centre stage following the Gershon Review (which identified a range of ways in which the government could release major resources through efficiency savings), it has rarely been out of the headlines.[34] The Government claims progress has been made and that it is on track to meet the efficiency targets identified in the Gershon Review, and in the 2005 PBR announced a total of £4.7 billion in efficiency gains at the end of September 2005.[35] There has been no shortage of alternative diagnoses and prescriptions. For example, the Conservative Party's *James Report*, issued in January 2005, claimed to identify £13 billion more potential savings than the Gershon Review,[36] while the *Bumper Book of Government Waste* identified 'billions' of pounds of public money which had been 'squandered' by the government.[37] Concerns over government progress were also highlighted in a 2006 report by the NAO, *Progress in Improving Government Efficiency*, which expressed reservations about whether the government was likely to meet its efficiency targets, arguing that the claims about progress that had been achieved should be regarded as 'provisional and subject to further verification'. It also warned that there was a risk that 'efficiency gains are accompanied by unintended falls in the quality of service'.[38]

5.11 Given what it perceives as the problems surrounding the issue of efficiency, the CBI called for a 'profoundly different approach' to achieving value for money. Its director Sir Digby Jones argued that there should be a standing version of the Gershon Review of public sector efficiency at arms length to government, staffed by specialists from the industry and academia, to provide permanent challenge to government on value for money.[39] However, this proposal has not been taken up by

---

[34] Gershon, P. (2004) *Releasing Resources to the Front Line: Independent Review of Public Sector Efficiency.*
[35] House of Commons Hansard, 2 March 2006, Col. 382.
[36] Conservative Party (2005) *The James Review of Tax Payer Value.*
[37] Elliot, M & Rotherham, L. (2006) *The Bumper Book of Government Waste*, Harriman House: London.
[38] NAO (2005-06) *Progress in Improving Government Efficiency*, HC 802.
[39] *Financial Times*, June 6 2005.

the Government and has also been rejected by PAC member Richard Bacon MP, who argues that the necessary work is already covered by the PAC. **Nevertheless, this issue of overall government efficiency makes it all the more pressing that PAC recommendations be systematically followed up and for the problems and solutions identified in the committee's value for money reports to be translated into wider lessons – both for government in carrying out its work and for Parliament in conducting its scrutiny of that work.**

The case for reform

5.12 The true test of the PAC's value is whether its work makes a real difference to public services and promoting financial efficiency within government. Detailed monitoring of action is one important element in assessing the outcomes achieved. Yet there is another step beyond simple monitoring; evaluation of recommendations can, if done badly, end up as a mechanistic 'box-ticking' exercise. It seems apparent that the vast majority of recommendations from the PAC are accepted, certainly in the sense that they are not formally rejected by government. The more fundamental question is whether long term improvements in outcomes are achieved, wider lessons are learned and mistakes not repeated. It is this step change that should be the focus of Parliament's efforts. **There should be a move towards a deeper notion of accountability – to ensure that individual lessons are translated into general reforms of public institutions that are found to be flawed.**

5.13 The NAO already has systems in place to monitor the recommendations made by them and the PAC and to track their implementation. A proportion of its value for money studies, up to 20 per cent in a given year, checks how effectively departments have implemented recommendations by the PAC. Examples in the past year include financial management in the EU, Ministry of Defence Major Projects Report plus financial audit work to follow up action on PAC recommendations on issues such as tax credits and benefits payments. The NAO recognises that by ensuring that 'its programme is flexible and responds to emerging issues of public and Parliamentary interest, it is not therefore always practical to formally follow up every report or, where we do so, to prescribe a timetable'. **Nonetheless, one recurring theme raised with us is that there should be a more co-ordinated approach to follow up the work of the PAC. The main criticism raised is that the issues uncovered by the NAO and the recommendations for changes made by the PAC do not necessarily have any tangible impact on the way that government operates.**

5.14 There is a danger with the current framework of scrutiny arrangements that the various parties involved – the audit bodies, Parliament and its committees as well as government – all have an interest in maintaining that the work they carry out is adequate and any impetus for change is limited. In this context, who challenges this and scrutinises the scrutineers? **Indeed, systems which can legitimately point to some success and effectiveness may be more resistant to change, and become more prone to complacency, than those whose faults are widely recognised.** Although it is evident that the current architecture of the NAO and PAC delivers significant benefits, many commentators contend that considerably more could be achieved.

Options for reform

5.15 The key to improving the effectiveness of Parliament's scrutiny work in this area is ensuring that its work has made a difference and that government has listened and acted upon recommendations. Follow-up systems are crucial. We identify a range of conclusions and options for reform.

5.16 Follow-up of PAC recommendations should not be haphazard but happen automatically. **One option would be to introduce a regular trigger for follow-up of NAO/PAC reports. As a general guide this could be set at 18 months or two years after the recommendations were first made, but could be extended or shortened where appropriate.** The key issue is not the exact timing of the review. A prescriptive approach would not be suitable in all cases. Some reports on emergency or critical issues might require a shorter timescale for review; others may take longer to ensure that changes have had time to bed down. The key point is that there should be an expectation and assumption that if the NAO/PAC have reported on a subject, then there will be a review or inquiry to find out what has happened since, whether change has been achieved and whether it has led to improvements. The timescale of 18 months to two years would provide a framework to guide work in this area. Furthermore, the knowledge that reports and specific recommendations are likely to be more closely monitored and reviewed may encourage better implementation measures by departments.

5.17 Another option, put forward by Edward Davey MP, is that the PAC should develop its own systems of auditing progress on recommendations. He argued that to assist in this, departments should be required not just to answer a PAC report, but also to publish at least one progress report perhaps one year later that the NAO can review. At least one further day should be made available for Parliament to look at PAC reports, including the annual report on progress achieved on its recommendations.[40]

---

[40] Davey E (ibid), p. 18.

Department select committees and financial scrutiny

5.18 However, given the limits on the PAC's capacity, (it produces over 50 reports a year), it would not be possible for it to undertake systematic follow-up of such a large number of reports. Instead, primary location of such follow-up work should lie with the departmental select committees. One of the functions that select committees have traditionally undertaken is scrutinising the effects of government expenditure and public services. The standing orders governing Commons departmental select committees give them powers to examine the expenditure of relevant government departments and associated public bodies.

5.19 In our interim report, *Inside the Counting House*, we drew attention to recent changes to the work of select committees that have strengthened their performance. We noted the changes introduced in 2002 which led to the adoption of 'core tasks' to guide the work of select committees. These tasks included 'To examine and report on Main Estimates, annual expenditure and annual resource accounts'. We concluded that 'since then, select committee scrutiny of departmental expenditure has become more systematic and more committees now undertake annual inquiries into relevant departmental reports'. Gwyneth Dunwoody MP noted the collective impact of these changes in evidence to this inquiry:

Select committees have begun to organise their work in a more structured way which enables them over the course of a parliamentary year to consider various aspects of the work and accounts of the departments that they monitor.

5.20 Select committees already work on a broad range of areas and it is inevitable that financial matters may not always command the highest priority. **One way of creating more capacity for select committees to perform financial scrutiny was proposed by the Hansard Society Scrutiny Commission, which recommended that each departmental select committee should pilot and evaluate a new form of committee, a Finance and Audit Sub-Committee.** As was discussed in section 4.18, such a sub-committee should consider, for example, estimates and departmental allocations, audit and value-for-money inquiries, PSAs, performance indicators and outcomes. It would also be the prime location for work to follow up NAO and PAC reports within a departmental select committee setting.

5.21 Even if finance and audit sub-committees were not established, it is important that select committees as a whole should be willing to conduct further inquiries on previously published NAO and PAC reports, using these reports as the starting point for more detailed examination and deliberation. While there is a danger that there might be little incentive or enthusiasm for other committees to follow up NAO work, in reality the reports provide material that would enhance the scrutiny work of the relevant committees. There are already examples of this sort of work, such as the February 2006 report of the Foreign Affairs Committee, which questioned the Foreign and Commonwealth Office's progress on a range of NAO recommendations.[41]

5.22 Departmental select committees are ideally placed to monitor the progress of recommendations made by the PAC within their subject area to assess whether the government has acted on its promises and whether such reforms have been effective. **One way to assist this process would be for DARs to include a specific section on progress taken in implementing the recommendations of NAO/PAC reports. Select committees should urge their relevant departments to provide this information.** Also, to promote more consistency across select committees, greater efforts should be made to share good practice in follow-up between select committees, for example by looking at joint themes, avoiding overlap and duplication and concentrating on the improvement agenda. Follow-up could be undertaken in conjunction with external bodies; for example, relevant inspectorates or institutes in the field could be asked to undertake evaluations to be submitted to parliamentary committees. Another option, if departmental select committees were not able to follow-up NAO/PAC reports, would be to have **committees in the House of Lords, which could be given greater access to NAO/ PAC reports to monitor whether progress has been made.** (For a further discussion of the role of the House of Lords on financial matters see section 10.)

Box C: Follow-up of PAC recommendations – a case study.[42]

A comparative study of the work of audit committees by University College London's Constitution Unit concluded 'the most systematic follow-up arrangements we found in this study are those of British Columbia, where procedures have been put in place to coordinate the actions of the PAC (by re-calling witnesses) and the Audit (by follow-up audits).'[43] Some of the key elements of the process include:

---

[41] Foreign Affairs Committee (2005-6) *Annual Report*, HC 903.
[42] The case study is based on information obtained from a Constitution Unit report for the Audit Committee of the Scottish Parliament. See Gay, O. & Winetrobe, B. (2003) *Parliamentary Audit: the Audit Committee in Comparative Context* (Constitution Unit: University College London).
[43] Gay, O. & Winetrobe, B. (Ibid)

- Following its appearance before the PAC, an audited body is asked to provide a progress update to the Office of the Auditor General (OAG) within a fixed period of time (usually five months).
- The written responses are reviewed by the OAG (to ensure that information provided on progress reported is a fair description) and disseminated by the Office of the Clerk of Committees to each committee member. The committee may request representatives of the audited body to attend an oral evidence session or submit a further written response.

Joined up work

5.23 One of the recurring themes throughout discussion of this subject is the need for greater joined up activity. This area encompasses both joined up work across issues and joined up work across different agencies. On this latter issue, the need for improved co-ordination has been recognised by the establishment of a Public Audit Forum (PAF) to 'provide a strategic focus on issues cutting across the work of the national audit bodies'. While the forum's main role is consultative and advisory (it does not include the power to direct the various agencies), its twice yearly meetings provide the heads of the various public audit agencies (the NAO, the Northern Ireland Audit Office, the Audit Commission, Audit Scotland and the Accounts Commission for Scotland, and the Auditor General for Wales) with the opportunity to consider common problems, disseminate good practice, and thereby enhance the effectiveness of their work. The various audit bodies also make extensive use of private sector financial management and accountancy expertise. The NAO noted in its submission that:

We work closely with other auditors and organisations involved in assessing and improving public services. The NAO are signatories to the Healthcare Concordat which aims to ensure a streamlined and strategic approach to the examination of health services. The NAO is uniquely placed to report to Parliament the results of co-operative work spanning the breadth of public expenditure. For example, the Comptroller and Auditor General's Report to Parliament in June 2005, Financial Management in the NHS, was prepared jointly by the NAO and the Audit Commission.

5.24 There has been progress on scrutiny of the link between input and output, through joint work by the NAO and Audit Commission which links the effect of top level policy with frontline services.[44] This joint work has increased in recent years. More such work by the NAO and the Audit Commission would be welcome. Co-ordination in the work of these bodies is essential firstly, to share good practice when it comes to carrying out public audit. Secondly, joined up working is needed to offer a complete picture of government expenditure and to enable more fully the bodies' assessment of what is happening. The PAC has been increasingly looking at cross cutting issues. A recent report looked at the management of public services over a 10 year period and identified seven key areas for improvement that emerged over this period. These included better planning, stronger project management, reduction of bureaucracy and complexity, and tackling fraud.[45] **Such a cross cutting approach is important in providing the fullest evidence on which Parliament can exact accountability from government.**

Box D: Supreme Auditing Institutions: some international comparisons

We set out below some international examples of Supreme Auditing Institutions, the bodies charged with carrying out the state audit.

The United States

- The Government Accountability Office (GAO) is an independent agency in the legislative branch of the federal government, charged with examining the use of federal funds, evaluating federal programmes and activities and providing information, analyses, recommendations and other assistance to help Congress make effective policy, funding and oversight decisions.

- The GAO has a statutory obligation to respond to requests from Congressional Committees and senior leaders of the parties in both Houses. This forms around 90 per cent of the GAO's work; the remainder is self initiated.

- There is no PAC equivalent in the US. GAO officials give evidence to Congressional Committees on more than 200 occasions each year. US

---

[44] The Audit Commission and the NAO also recently published a report with the Health Care Commission on Childhood Obesity. See NAO (2006) *Tackling Child Obesity - First Steps, Report of a joint study by the Healthcare Commission, the National Audit Office and the Audit Commission.*
[45] PAC (2005-06) *Achieving Value for Money in the Delivery of Public Services*, HC 742.

- Congressional Committees have their own staff who will normally conduct the preliminary investigations.
- Agencies must respond to Congress on GAO recommendations whether they implement them or not.
- The GAO monitor the implementation of recommendations in conjunction with the relevant Committee or the appropriate sub committee of the Appropriations Committee. The GAO aims to monitor the progress of recommendations for four years after they have been issued.

Australia

- The Australian National Audit Office (ANAO) is an independent public sector agency headed by the Auditor General.
- The ANAO works closely with the Joint Committee of Public Accounts and Audit (JCPAA), which is comprised of members from the House and the Senate.
- The JCPAA considers reports from the ANAO and can initiate inquiries into other matters. The committee has a professional secretariat supplemented by secondees from the ANAO, the Department of Finance and Consultants.
- The ANAO takes into account the view of the JCPAA and parliamentarians in planning its work: in 2004-05 it produced five performance audits in response to suggestions from committees or members.
- The ANAO periodically conducts follow-up performance audits on whether recommendations from previous reports have been implemented.

New Zealand

- The Auditor General is an officer of Parliament. The Audit General's office is organised into two units: the Office of the Auditor General (OAG) which carries out performance audits and parliamentary reporting and Audit New Zealand which carries out the financial audit of accounts
- There is no PAC equivalent in New Zealand: relevant select committees consider the OAG's performance audit reports.
- The OAG also provides assistance to select committees on both estimates and financial reviews – producing around 60-70 reports or briefings a year.

Section 6

The Role of the Audit Commission

6.1 The Audit Commission (AC) is an independent public body which is responsible for auditing many of the most important public services, including local government, certain front-line and local health services, housing and fire and rescue services. One notable feature about the status of the AC is that, although it makes contributions to select committees on financial management and scrutiny issues, it does not have a formal relationship with a select committee, as is the case with the NAO and the PAC. In 2000, the Environment Transport and Regional Affairs Committee (ETRA) in its report, *Audit Commission*, cited a proposal by the then PAC chairman, David Davis MP, that a new select committee should be established to consider and report on the work of the Audit Commission.[46] The Committee, however, did not endorse this proposal, believing that services provided by local authorities should be accountable to local electorates and that Parliament should not attempt, even indirectly, to hold these accountable.[47]

6.2 The 2001 Hansard Society Scrutiny Commission report did not share the Committee's analysis, arguing that 'Many of the services currently under the remit of the Audit Commission, most notably health and police services, are not directly provided by locally elected authorities and a strong case could be made for parliamentary oversight' and proposed that the Audit Commission should report directly to the relevant departmental select committees. However, this recommendation was not taken forward by the Government. Nevertheless, this issue has not gone away. Most obviously, enormous amounts of central government funding are given to local authorities; in 2006-07 the government will provide local authorities in England with in excess of £120 billion of public money.[48] While local forms of accountability should exist for the actions and expenditure of local government, the considerable central government funds deployed by government, and the huge role that local services have in delivering the services mandated in top level policy, make systematic parliamentary scrutiny essential.

6.3 In its evidence to this inquiry, the Audit Commission noted that it: *Has made several contributions to select committees on financial management and*

---

[46] ETRA (1999-2000) *Audit Commission*, HC174-I.
[47] ETRA (ibid) para 74.
[48] House of Commons Hansard, 15 February 2006, Col. 667.

scrutiny and we are pleased that many of our recommendations have been taken forward. We welcome the opportunity to contribute to these committees as a way of influencing public policy development in this area. However, unlike the NAO's statutory relationship with the PAC, the Commission does not have a formal process whereby our findings are looked at by the relevant select committee.

6.4 There is a strong case for believing that the important areas audited and scrutinised by the AC would benefit from closer consideration by parliamentary committees. As noted, one option would be to have a direct relationship with a parliamentary committee, along the lines of the NAO/PAC. Alternatively, a different approach could be taken, especially as comparing the NAO and the AC is not a matter of comparing like with like. Crucially, unlike the NAO, the AC has a sponsoring government department, the Office for Communities and Local Government. Furthermore, much of the AC's work is cross-cutting, and so it may not be suitable for it to be restricted to links with one particular committee and it may be more suitable for the AC to develop closer links with the relevant committees. It would be beneficial if there was a more systematic basis for the relevant select committees to consider AC reports. **Rather than the somewhat piecemeal approach which Parliament takes to the work of the AC, select committees should seek to forge closer relationships with the Commission and make greater use of its evidence to strengthen their work. We recommend that the appropriate select committees consider AC reports on a more systematic basis.**

6.5 Additionally, in its evidence, the AC pointed to weaknesses in the current auditing system. For example, it noted the absence of a requirement for local authorities to have audit committees and to produce annual reports. In particular, the AC drew attention to its view that its effectiveness is also limited by the increasingly prominent role played by local authority-owned companies in local government, and yet such companies cannot be audited by the AC. In its evidence, the AC made the case for an extension in its remit in this area, noting that: 'The effectiveness of our oversight of public expenditure is diminished because we do not audit the increasing number of companies that are wholly owned by our audited bodies.' The AC pointed out that Lord Sharman, in his 2001 report to the Government, *Holding to Account*, recommended that in addition to establishing arrangements to enable the C&AG to audit NDPBs, and subsidiaries of NDPBs set up as companies, similar arrangements should also be introduced for the audit of local government and for the Auditor General for Scotland and the Auditor General for Wales. **We endorse the Audit Commission's proposal that consideration should be given to extending the Audit Commission's powers to appoint auditors to local authority-owned companies.**

Section 7

Audit and Devolution

7.1 As part of the post-devolution constitutional settlement, a number of changes to the public audit regimes in Scotland and Wales were introduced.

The Wales Audit Office

7.2 Responsibility for auditing the public sector in Wales lies with the Wales Audit Office (WAO). Established in 2005, the WAO monitors the annual spending of the National Assembly for Wales and other public sector bodies, and assesses the economy, efficiency and effectiveness with which the Assembly uses its resources to carry out its functions. Unlike in Westminster, the WAO's examinations cover not only the Assembly and Assembly Sponsored Public Bodies but also local NHS bodies and further and higher education institutions. These bodies had, prior to the passage of the Public Audit (Wales) Act 2004, been under the remit of the Audit Commission.

7.3 When the joined up approach to public audit was adopted in Wales, it was welcomed by the Chartered Institute of Public Finance and Accountancy (CIPFA), which argued that it would have a beneficial impact on public sector bodies in Wales through 'efficiencies and through the impact of joined up planning in reducing the regulatory burden'.[49] However the Welsh Local Government Association expressed some concerns that it could lead to a 'one size fits all' methodology, 'which ignores the very real different operational environments facing public sector organisations in the various spheres of activity'.[50]

7.4 The reports of the WAO are presented to the National Assembly's Audit Committee, which carries out specific inquiries into issues of interest or concern arising from these reports, without questioning the merits of policy objectives of the body under review. While control over what issues to examine lies with the WAO, the Auditor General presents the committee with an annual memorandum setting out the Assembly's proposed programme of value for money examinations, to enable the Committee to have active input on the issues to be considered.

---

[49] CIPFA, *Response to the Wales Office Draft Public Audit* (Wales) Bill.
[50] Welsh Affairs Committee (2002-03) *Draft Public Audit (Wales) Bill*, HC 763.

7.5 In its evidence to this inquiry, the Society of Welsh Treasurers argued that the scrutiny system in Wales also benefits from joined up work between members of the National Assembly and local government representatives:

Regular meetings are held on financial matters between officers of the Assembly and officers of the [local] Councils together with the Welsh Local Government Association. Similar regular meetings are also held between elected representatives. This hopefully allows the Assembly to be far more aware of the issues in local government and local government to be better informed and participate in forming central policies. The exchange of proper and timely information is a prerequisite of effective policy.

Audit Scotland

7.6 In Scotland the Auditor General (AG) and the Accounts Commission are responsible for carrying out the public audit. The AG, an independent examiner who reports to the Scottish Parliament, scrutinises departments of the Scottish Executive and other bodies including NHS boards, further education colleges, government agencies and non-departmental public bodies. The Accounts Commission, which is independent of local councils and government, makes reports and recommendations to Scottish Ministers. It appoints auditors to Scotland's councils and joint boards and helps them manage their resources effectively and efficiently.

7.7 Audit Scotland provides services to both the Auditor General and the Accounts Commission and oversees the audits of around 200 public bodies across Scotland, including 19 Executive departments and agencies, local authorities, NHS trusts and further education colleges, which are together responsible for spending over £26 billion pounds a year. The majority of the audits are carried out by staff at Audit Scotland, while the rest are carried out by firms of appointed auditors. In addition to audit reports, Audit Scotland monitors how different sectors, organisations or programmes perform during the financial year.

7.8 While any subject committee in the Scottish Parliament has the power to examine value for money issues, in practice such work is carried out by the Audit Committee. The Committee may consider and report on accounts laid before the Parliament. It may also examine reports of the AG and other documents relating to financial control, accounting or auditing relating to public expenditure that are laid before it. In practice the Committee only undertakes inquiries into reports by the Auditor General, which are based on work carried out by Audit Scotland. The auditing arrangements in Scotland have been subject to some criticism. For example, CIPFA has argued 'that there is benefit from having more than one public audit agency and a distinct scope of activities for these bodies'.[51] In addition, as the Accounts Commission does not report to the Scottish Parliament, significant amounts of public finances are not subject to parliamentary scrutiny.

7.9 The joined up approach adopted by both the Wales Audit Office and Audit Scotland (whereby the bodies scrutinise both central and local government) are believed by some to promote more effective parliamentary scrutiny by offering a more complete picture of public finances and also enabling analysis of the implications that the top level policy has on the ground and in front-line services. **They point to, at the very least, the need for continued joint work by the NAO and the Audit Commission. Given that there are now a range of different arrangements within the UK, it is important that Westminster learns any lessons and good practice from Wales and Scotland.**

---

[51] CIPFA, Comments on 'A Financial Framework for the Scottish Parliament', a consultation paper by the Scottish Executive. Available at www.cipfa.org.uk .

Section 8

The Private Finance Initiative

8.1 The way that government spends money and delivers services has changed dramatically in recent years, at a rate which shows no signs of slowing. Such changes place a responsibility on both government and Parliament to ensure that up to date mechanisms are in place to ensure full accountability. One notable example of a new model of expenditure, which has presented a challenge to both government and Parliament, involves Private Finance Initiatives (PFI).

8.2 PFIs refer to the legal contracts by which private companies are involved in the provision of public services and are the most well known form of Public Private Partnerships. Since their introduction in 1992, the initiatives have been used for an increasingly wide range of public service projects, including new hospitals, prisons, transport infrastructure and government buildings. Over 700 PFI projects with a total value of £46 billion have been signed by the government (across over 20 different sectors) to date and following the 2006 Budget the use of such investment is set to increase.

8.3 Although its outcomes in terms of efficiency and value for money have been questioned from some sources,[52] the government believes that PFI encourages value for money in public expenditure (it is argued that the risk borne by PFI providers gives them an incentive to be efficient and to deliver on time) and transfers risk to the private sector.[53] PFI contracts vary enormously in terms of sector and type of work involved. However the commercial confidentiality accorded to private partners in these contracts appears to pose a particular challenge for effective parliamentary scrutiny. In evidence to this inquiry, Gwyneth Dunwoody MP, noting her experiences as chair of the Transport Committee, described as 'wholly unacceptable' the lack of information on PFI partners available to select committee inquiries:

The area in which we have encountered the greatest difficulty in scrutinising the work of the Department is the Private Finance Initiative or Public Private Partnerships... the number of occasions on which we were informed that the figures we were seeking were unavailable due to commercial confidentiality became more than a joke...

---

[52] See UNISON (2005) *A Policy Built on Sand.*
[53] HM Treasury (2006) *PFI: Strengthening Long-Term Partnerships.*

8.4 She further argued that the continued lack of information placed 'severe constraints upon committees' ability to inquire into the viability and value for money of such schemes, particularly if the facts are confidential'. Other commentators have suggested that PFI contracts provide government with 'a means of escaping' effective parliamentary scrutiny as, in certain circumstances, the liabilities of PFI contracts are excluded from public sector liabilities and estimates.[54] This has been denied by the government which claims, 'The accounting treatment of a PFI project on a departmental balance sheet, and its reflection as an asset in the national accounts, plays no part in the government's decision about when to use PFI. That decision is based on value for money.'[55]

8.5 Parliamentary scrutiny of PFI projects is largely conducted by the NAO, which has produced over 50 reports on the initiatives since they were first introduced. The reports consider how individual contracts were awarded, how deals are working in practice and thematic issues such as refinancing or managing PFI relationships. Recommendations are presented to the PAC and also to relevant government departments to enable them to draw lessons. Research by the NAO has shown that its work on PFI projects has saved the taxpayer £750 million in six years. For example, a report on the refinancing of the Fazakerley Prison PFI contract led to new guidelines on how PFI contracts should be drawn up and implemented.[56]

8.6 Nevertheless, the NAO's evidence to this inquiry pointed to the complexity of the accounting methods involved in PFI contracts:

It is clear that different interpretations of the accounting guidance have been applied to projects in different parts of the public sector. This may have an impact on the Whole of Government Accounts incorporating the local government and health sectors.

To address this problem the C&AG has been working with the Treasury and other audit bodies to investigate the factors behind 'the seemingly inconsistent treatments and to consider whether changes to the guidance are necessary'. However, the way that Parliament itself scrutinises PFI projects has also been subject to criticism. According to McEldowney and Lee:

Parliamentary scrutiny of PFI has been ad hoc – mainly relying on the NAO to draw attention to any impropriety... Select committee scrutiny tends to be spasmodic and reactive... PFI arrangements set new challenges for Parliament in examining a

---

[54] See Shaoul, J. (2004) 'A critical appraisal of the private finance initiative: selecting a financial method or allocating economic wealth?', *Critical Perspectives on Accounting*.

[55] HM Treasury (March 2006) PFI: *Strengthening Long-Term Partnerships*, p. 23.

[56] For further information see a recent report by the PAC, reviewing the impact of NAO/PAC work over a 10 year period. PAC, *Achieving Value for Money in the Delivery of Public Services*, HC 742.

technically complex and difficult subject.[57]

8.7 Our inquiry points to the need for more systematic parliamentary scrutiny, which is pro-active rather than reactive and seeks to ensure that lessons learnt from mistakes are translated into improvements in PFI systems. In particular, **consideration of PFI projects by departmental and other select committees should be extended,** and there should be greater follow-up on recommendations previously made. Given the complexity of the issues involved in PFI contracts, the NAO's support to committees other than the PAC should be extended in this area.

8.8 Our inquiry also points to the need for much greater transparency regarding the private partners in PFI contracts. Richard Bacon MP stressed the need to account for public funds should override concerns over 'corporate confidentiality'.[58] He pointed to the considerable benefits that private companies gain through their involvement in PFI projects and argued that if they entered into such contracts they have to accept the need for greater disclosure. **PFI contracts should be subject to full select committee scrutiny and 'commercial confidentiality' should not be used to block full parliamentary scrutiny.** Identifying the best way to inject better transparency in the use of PFI is beyond the scope of our inquiry and requires a comprehensive review by government or an inquiry by Parliament. However, one idea that was put to us would be for **PFI contracts to include a requirement for the private partner to share information, not only with public auditing bodies, but with parliamentary committees as well.**

8.9 The problems associated with PFI point to the broader question of how parliamentary scrutiny can keep pace with changes to the way government operates. PFIs are far from being the only new initiative to challenge Parliament's system of scrutiny. It is essential that Parliament has a mechanism to ensure its system of financial scrutiny recognises and responds to these changes, if it is to conduct its work as rigorously and effectively as possible. (We consider how this could take place in section 11.)

---

[57] McEldowney, J. & Lee, C. (ibid) p. 83.
[58] See Richard Bacon's speech on 'Improving value for money for taxpayers in PFI projects', given to the City Forum in June 2004. A full transcript of the speech is available at www.richardbacon.org.uk.

Section 9

Scrutiny of European Union Expenditure

9.1 The European Union is responsible for spending over £80 billion pounds of public money a year (approximately one per cent of the gross national product of each member state), funded through a combination of contributions from member states and its 'own resources'.[59] Activities funded in the 25 member states range from agriculture and fisheries to employment and social policy, and humanitarian aid for non-EU countries.

9.2 There are a number of mechanisms for Parliament to monitor and scrutinise the UK's contributions to the European Union as well as the way that the EU spends and manages the money it raises. EU funds received by the UK public sector pass in the first instance through the accounts of government departments and are therefore audited, and subject to value for money examinations, by the NAO. However, overall responsibility for auditing the collection and spending of EU funds lies with the European Court of Auditors (ECA). The court examines whether financial operations have been properly recorded, legally and regularly executed and managed to ensure 'economy, efficiency and effectiveness'. In carrying out this role it works with Supreme Auditing Institutions and government departments in member countries.

9.3 To enable effective parliamentary scrutiny of EU finances, the NAO produces an annual report entitled *Financial Management in the European Union* which has on occasion formed the basis of a PAC report. The report summarises the ECA's review of community accounts and comments on other developments in EU financial management. The importance of NAO work in this area was highlighted in a recent debate in the Commons on financial management in the EU.[60]

9.4 Controversy has accompanied the work of the ECA, which has never given a positive Statement of Assurance on Community Accounts since the statements were first introduced in 1994. In November 2005 the Court rejected the EU's annual accounts for the 11th consecutive time, arguing 'that the vast majority of the payment budget was again materially affected by errors of legality and regularity'. It

---

[59] 'Own resources' include custom duties on imports, agricultural levies, contributions from Member States based on a proportion of their Gross National Income and a notional rate of one per cent VAT applied to a range of goods and services in all Member States.

[60] House of Commons Hansard, 7 March 2006, Col. 747- 793.

found that half the projects approved by the European Commission were inadequately monitored, that the situation represented 'no major improvement' and was largely due to 'over-declaration of costs, declarations of ineligible costs or absence of supporting documentation'. More positively, however, a recent report from the NAO noted that some progress had been in this area, notably the development of a road map towards a positive statement of assurance, devised during the United Kingdom's Presidency of the Union. [61]

9.5 In 2003 the NAO announced it would carry out increased scrutiny of EU spending, 'to ensure that the revenues and expenditures of the EU are audited to international accounting standards'. Given the significant amount of UK public money that is expended on the EU, the lack of accountability within the Union should be a cause of great concern, within and outside Parliament. **While several debates on the issue have taken place, more consistent pressure on government to seek a solution to the crisis, including through the Council of Ministers, should be applied by Parliament.**

9.6 The question also remains of how further scrutiny of spending by the European Union could be conducted within the Westminster Parliament. Effective scrutiny is particularly crucial given the large (and increasing) financial contributions made by the United Kingdom to the EU. Given the large number of reports already produced by the PAC, one option would be for **more financial scrutiny work, supported by the NAO, to be conducted by the House of Commons European Scrutiny Committee (ESC) and the House of Lords European Union Committee (EUC).** The EUC in particular has great potential in this area (the ESC is widely considered to be overburdened). The Hansard Society's recent briefing paper on scrutiny of European Union business noted the 'highly effective scrutiny work' undertaken by the Committee, pointing out that unlike its Commons equivalent it is able to consider fewer documents in greater depth, through the work of its seven sub committees.[62]

9.7 The sub-committee on Economic and Financial Affairs and Trade (Sub Committee A) already produces an annual report on the European Commission's draft budget, based on oral evidence taken from the government ahead of the first reading of the Budget in the Council. According to the committee 'taking evidence from the government at such an early stage in the budgetary process is the most effective way to fulfil our parliamentary obligation to scrutinise EU legislation, and to increase accountability and transparency'. **One possibility would be for further**

---

[61] NAO (2006) *Financial Management of the European Union.*
[62] Hansard Society (2006) *Scrutiny of European Union Business: Issues in Law Making Paper 8,* Hansard Society: London.

financial scrutiny to be conducted by this Committee, supported by the NAO. As noted earlier, while there are some concerns about the Lords' involvement in authorising expenditure, this should not prevent the House from being actively involved in scrutiny of past expenditure. Indeed the expertise of members of the Lords (members of the EUC sub committees are chosen on the basis of their expertise and there is reportedly a waiting list to join the committee) has the potential to greatly strengthen the scrutiny work of Parliament.

9.8 In March 2005 the Commons Modernisation Committee published a report on *Scrutiny of European Business* which made a range of recommendations to strengthen the system.[63] Its proposals including the establishment of a Joint Grand Committee of both Houses, the publication of an annual white paper on forthcoming EU legislation, and regular progress reports. We welcome the Committee's recommendations, to which, at the time of writing, the Government has not yet responded. The Joint Committee would provide an ideal forum for further financial scrutiny of European spending plans and expenditure.

---

[63] Modernisation Committee (2004-05) *Scrutiny of European Business*, HC 465 I-II.

Section 10

The Role of the House of Lords

10.1 It is widely assumed that when it comes to financial matters, the House of Lords merely endorses what the Commons has agreed to, and does not get involved in debates regarding financial policy or with implications on government spending. The financial powers of the Upper House are certainly constrained, firstly by ancient 'rights and privileges' of the Commons (established in the 17th century) and statutorily by the terms of the Parliament Act 1911. As a result, the Lords are prevented from initiating or amending any legislation relating to the granting of supply or the imposition of tax.

10.2 However, there are no conventions or procedures that prevent members of the House of Lords from expressing their opinion on public spending or taxation, whether by resolution or in debate, or by carrying out scrutiny within select committees. The rules governing this issue state that the Lords can 'express their opinion upon public expenditure, and the method of taxation and financial administration, both in debate and by resolution, and they have investigated these matters by their select committees'.[64]

10.3 In 2002, the Leaders Group on Working Practices within the Lords was set up to review new procedures. It considered how the House could have a more active role in considering the Finance Bill, without encroaching on the Commons' financial privileges. Its report recommended that the House establish a permanent sub-committee within the Economic Affairs Committee (EAC), to consider the Bill.[65] It stressed that the Committee should focus on scrutinising tax administration and clarifying proposals in the Bill, rather than on the incidence or level of taxation. The Committee, which was established with the unanimous agreement of the House, has since taken written and oral evidence from experts and officials, looked in detail at subjects such as stamp duty and small business taxation, and issued regular reports. In evidence Lord Wakeham (chairman of the EAC but writing to this inquiry in a personal capacity), noted:

The Finance Bill Sub-Committee had a somewhat difficult birth. Painful memories of the budget crisis of 1911 still hovered perhaps in some quarters, leading to what the

---

[64] Erskine May (2004) *Parliamentary Practice*, 23rd Edition, p. 908.
[65] Leaders Group on Working Practices, (2002) *Report by the Group Appointed to Consider how the Working Practices of the House can be Improved, and to make Recommendation*, HL 111.

Liaison Committee delicately termed 'the sensitivities surrounding this initiative'. But it has survived to maturity and is clearly here to stay. It has made a constructive and helpful contribution to the evolving process of parliamentary consideration of Finance Bills. It is now time to consider a modest development in its role.

10.4 In previous sections we have outlined a number of options for greater involvement and activity by the House of Lords in financial scrutiny issues. One area would be the establishment of a Joint Committee of both Houses to look at tax administration, assuming that the principle of the financial precedence of the Commons is safeguarded and that its remit was confined solely to tax administration.

10.5 There is potential for the Lords to take a role in following up issues raised in previously published NAO and PAC reports. The common perception that the NAO is simply a resource designed for the sole use of the Commons is not quite as straightforward as it seems. The relevant legislation, the 1983 National Audit Act, states in relation to the Comptroller and Auditor General's (C&AG) value for money examinations, that the C&AG is to report to the House of Commons. It is the convention that the C&AG reports are considered first by the PAC. However, once these reports are published, they become available to both Houses. Therefore, the House of Lords would not be able to instruct the C&AG to undertake a particular function. (Indeed neither the Lords nor the Commons can instruct the C&AG to do anything, unless it is set down in statute.) However, the Lords can invite the C&AG to participate in a particular piece of work and, for example, the C&AG appeared last year before the Lords BBC Charter Review Select Committee.

10.6 Furthermore, there is no reason why the Lords cannot make use of C&AG reports once they have been laid in the House and published. However, because the 1983 Act refers to the C&AG reporting to the House of Commons, it is through this route that his work becomes available to the Lords, rather than the C&AG reporting directly to the Lords. There is therefore a distinction between reporting to the Lords and reports being made available to the Lords. It should also be noted that the main estimate relating to the NAO (presented to Parliament during the supply process) states the purpose of the NAO is to provide 'independent assurance to Parliament and other organisations on the management of public resources'. The crucial point is that the scrutiny functions of the Lords (whether at present or after a reform settlement) could be substantially strengthened by greater use of the specialist and expert reports of the NAO. **There is particular scope for the Lords to play a part in reviewing and following up previous NAO/PAC reports. Given**

the high quality of scrutiny carried out by the Lords in many areas and because of the wide range of expertise of its Members, it is clear that the Lords could play a much greater role in financial scrutiny matters.

House of Lords Reform

10.7 After many false starts and hesitant steps, it seems likely that a reformed second chamber will be established in the near future. One central theme put forward by reformers of all political viewpoints is that the reformed House should have a central role in seeking and obtaining accountability of government. **As we have argued, financial scrutiny and accountability issues go to the heart of the relationship between government and Parliament. Therefore, it is essential that the reformed Lords should have an important input into this work, most particularly on the scrutiny of past government expenditure.**

Section 11

Developing Good Practice

11.1 Parliamentarians in general, and MPs in particular, are first and foremost politicians and cannot be expected to be experts in financial scrutiny. However, this does not mean that the parliamentary system as a whole should not aspire to the most effective scrutiny methods. It is clear from evidence we have received that there is concern, even confusion, about the context and purpose of some of this scrutiny work. On the one hand, the issues of taxation and expenditure go to the heart of some of the most intensely political debates about the role and scope of the state. On the other, financial scrutiny is seen as the dry and analytical consideration of facts and figures. Therefore, the political battle between government and opposition can sometimes conflict with the requirement for Parliament to carry out dispassionate analysis of government finance.

11.2 It is now standard practice for all organisations (whether public or private) to establish guidelines for good practice in their work. If a body decides that they should carry out a certain project, consideration is given to why the work is being carried out, what it hopes to achieve and how outcomes can be monitored and evaluated. While some commentators may disparage the alleged 'faddishness' of management techniques, the reason that their use is so widespread is that they are considered to be an effective tool to improve performance. The complexity of Parliament's work – and the sometimes conflicting pressures on parliamentarians – can make a uniform approach to scrutiny more difficult than in less overtly political forums. However, some extra consistency and analysis of its work would be welcome. The adoption of some core principles on financial scrutiny could help guide Parliament in carrying out work in this area; at the very least they could act as standards by which the quality of Parliament's financial scrutiny work could be measured.

11.3 The Centre for Public Scrutiny (CfPS) has published a *Good Scrutiny Guide* which defines a set of principles for the effective exercise of public accountability. Box E outlines the themes and mechanisms identified in the most recent guide, which, if applied in the parliamentary context, would strengthen its scrutiny and accountability functions. Parliament should consider whether it should adopt some similar principles for its scrutiny functions.

Box E: Centre for Public Scrutiny: The Good Scrutiny Guide[66]

The Centre for Public Scrutiny's Good Scrutiny Guide defines a set of principles for the effective exercise of public accountability. It identifies four principles of effective scrutiny that together form a 'good scrutiny cycle', through which 'critical friend' challenges lead to service improvement.

1. Good public scrutiny provides 'critical friend' challenge to executives and external agencies:

Effective scrutiny should offer constructive, robust and purposeful challenge. It will need to demonstrate:

- that opportunities are available for 'scrutineers' to question representatives of the executive on a regular basis, including ministers, senior civil servants, and any others with significant responsibility through contractual agreement;

- an evidence-based approach, independent of executive influence; and

- an appropriate balance between challenging, and maintaining constructive working relationships with the executive.

Those with financial responsibility should be able to point to the scrutiny function as a dependable and objective means to demonstrate their own accountability.

2. Good public scrutiny enables the voice and concerns of the public:

Scrutiny is carried out on behalf of the public as a safeguard on the exercise of power. However, truly effective scrutiny should do more than simply 'represent' the public voice; it should 'enable' it by ensuring an ongoing dialogue. To succeed in doing this a scrutiny function should:

- provide simple mechanisms to encourage and enable public participation in its work, which is more meaningful and less daunting than a simple 'call for evidence' or request for a question to be asked in the House of Commons;

---

[66] This section is based on evidence provided by the Centre for Public Scrutiny.

- offer a simple explanation of what an enquiry seeks to achieve. This may be to effect a tangible change in policy or resource allocation in the public interest, or to enhance the profile of a particular issue by raising and exploring it through public debate;

- take advantage of all opportunities to communicate the proposal, proceedings, and result of its work.

3. Good public scrutiny is carried out by 'independent minded governors' who lead and own the scrutiny role:

The scrutiny function should be carried out by independent and impartial 'non-executives', who act as standard bearers for good scrutiny as a mechanism for better accountability and perform a community leadership role by building evidence-based consensus around issues of public concern.

Achieving 'independence' is perhaps less problematic in the parliamentary arena than in the field of local government, where fewer members and smaller party groups can make the concept of an independent and objective voice more difficult to realise.

4. Good public scrutiny drives improvement in public services:

The concerns of scrutiny committees should be fed into a cycle of service improvement. In terms of financial accountability, success against this principle at the local authority level would need to consider how effectively the work of 'overview and scrutiny' is co-ordinated with the authority's regular cycle of planning, budgeting and performance measurement. In the parliamentary setting this role can be seen largely as the responsibility of departmental select committees and the PAC to make every effort to ensure that their work is adopted and acted upon by government.

11.4 We also provide an example of what the process of effective scrutiny should encompass. Box F provides an outline of the system prepared for this report by the government and public sector team at PricewaterhouseCoopers (PwC). Neither this example, nor the principles outlined by the CfPS, necessarily constitutes a blueprint to be adopted. **However, as Parliament frequently seeks to establish best practice in government and other bodies that it scrutinises, there is a strong case for arguing that its own work would benefit from the adoption of a framework of principles to guide and underpin its work.**

Box F: PricewaterhouseCoopers: Developing an effective scrutiny process

The development of an effective scrutiny process should exhibit the same best practice principles inherent within any robust system or framework. These principles are illustrated in the figure below, showing a simple seven-step approach to developing and maintaining a robust scrutiny process. Each step is explained below.

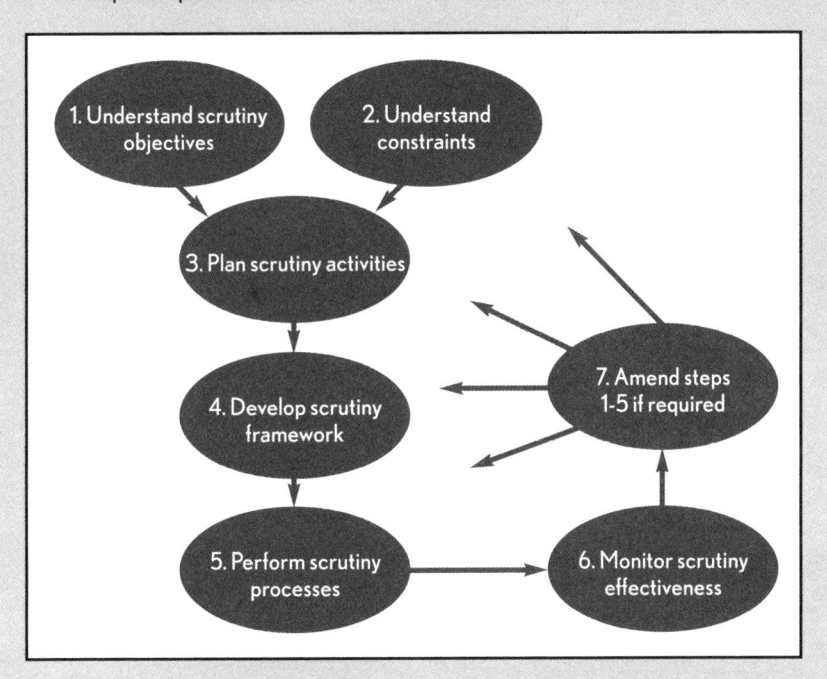

```
1. Understand scrutiny objectives
2. Understand constraints
3. Plan scrutiny activities
4. Develop scrutiny framework
5. Perform scrutiny processes
6. Monitor scrutiny effectiveness
7. Amend steps 1-5 if required
```

1. Understand scrutiny objectives

Why is scrutiny important? What is it trying to achieve? How will we know if it has been effective? The scrutiny process must be based on a common understanding of what it is intended to achieve, taking into account the policy context and the requirements of all relevant stakeholders. Without this understanding, it would be impossible to develop robust scrutiny processes, or to analyse the effectiveness of the activities comprising parliamentary scrutiny.

2. Understand constraints

It is equally important to identify the constraints affecting the scrutiny process. These could be political, as well as the common constraints of available resources and time. Established data reporting processes (content, timing etc) might also give rise to constraints in the scrutiny options.

3. Plan scrutiny activities

Planning is the crucial activity that identifies the approach to be taken to meet the objectives identified in step 1, within the constraints identified in step 2. This step can often prove difficult to coordinate, if there is disagreement over the objectives or if there is no natural mandate or authority over all the potential sources of scrutiny.

4. Develop scrutiny framework

The development of the scrutiny framework will require design of scrutiny processes, and allocation of these to one or more organisations or functions. Scrutiny process design should have regard to the standard elements inherent in any best practice process. These elements include clear objectives, due regard to efficiency, economy and effectiveness, and with continuous review and improvement cycles embedded at appropriate points. The organisations that will deliver the scrutiny must have sufficient capacity to perform the planned activities, including having appropriate experience, expertise, resources and available time. Where more than one organisation is involved, a key focus will be the integration and coherence of their respective scrutiny activities so that the overall objectives are met.

5. Perform scrutiny processes

This step features the implementation and operation of the scrutiny processes or activities identified in the plan. This is likely to include a range of different types of activity. Again, there is a need to ensure that the overall scrutiny processes, once implemented, deliver against the stated objectives.

6. Monitor scrutiny effectiveness

Periodically, the effectiveness of the scrutiny framework should be considered, to reassess if it is meeting the original objectives identified in step 1. This could be achieved through activities such as seeking confirmation from stakeholders that their needs are still being met, or by review of any apparent failings in scrutiny and assessment of whether lessons learned indicate a need for changes to the scrutiny process.

7. Amend steps 1-5 if required

The scrutiny process should be a constant loop, with appropriate amendments made to any of steps 1-5 if it is not fulfilling the objectives for which it has been designed.

Often, reviews to provide assurance that such a process is robust, concentrate only on steps 5 and 6 – analysing processes and their effectiveness, without revisiting and revalidating what these activities are intended to achieve. In addition, planning is often inadequate, especially if there are many different parties involved in the process, each with their own agenda and views on how they should operate. Therefore, to ensure the integrity, coherence and effectiveness of the system of scrutiny, all steps set out above must be examined.

11.5 **Parliament would benefit from a more systematic, and self-reflective approach to its financial scrutiny work. It should ensure that all the different processes and procedures are suitable for the purpose they are intended for and link together to offer a complete picture of government activity.** The models described above provide a guideline for how this could take place.

Section 12

Measuring Performance: Inputs and Outputs

12.1 A focus on the outputs of government activity is as central to effective scrutiny as the evaluation of the resources that have been expended (the inputs). The issue of outputs is relevant to our inquiry in two specific ways: firstly it is essential for Parliament to consider fully the outcomes of government expenditure, particularly in terms of their impact on public services and front-line delivery. At the same time it is essential for Parliament to adopt this output-focused approach when it assesses its own performance and determines how it can strengthen its scrutiny work.

12.2 It was suggested at our seminar that Parliament is not configured as an institution that deals with outputs. Procedures within Parliament are designed to deal primarily with inputs rather than outputs or the link between the two. This is a problem, as ignoring this link prevents MPs from developing a comprehensive understanding of the impact of public expenditure and why things go wrong. However, some participants disagreed, arguing that the link between inputs and outputs was being made in the work carried out by the NAO and the PAC, whose activities in determining 'the economy, efficiency and effectiveness' of government spending inevitably involves considering the outcomes of that spending.

12.3 Others felt that Parliament's inability to consider properly the impact of government's work was the product of debate hovering at the policy level – whether on health or education – rather than on assessing detailed financial matters and performance. Furthermore, failure to look at detailed financial matters also means that MPs tend to focus on new changes to the budget while frequently ignoring money previously allocated. In scrutinising government spending Parliament needs to ensure that in looking at new spending it does not neglect reviewing previously allocated expenditure. MPs need to look at what has been allocated previously – how it was used, whether it succeeded in achieving what was intended, and whether it could be better spent elsewhere.

12.4 A focus on outputs is also crucial when it comes to how Parliament assesses its own work. As one of the ultimate aims of scrutiny of government finance is to improve the quality of services being delivered to the public, it is essential for Parliament to be self-reflective and to be able to assess whether its scrutiny of government is as rigorous and effective as possible and whether its work is resulting in tangible improvements.

Recent innovations

12.5 Effective financial scrutiny requires transparent and appropriate measures of input and output. Over the past few years the government has introduced a range of innovations designed to increase transparency of the financial and expenditure systems, and to enable more effective assessment of the outputs of government activity. The introduction of Public Service Agreements (PSAs) and, more recently, Whole of Government Accounts and the full implementation of Resource Accounting and Budgeting (RAB) are some of the most notable. (For a description of these changes see *Inside the Counting House*.)

12.6 The success of these innovations depends in part on the reaction of parliamentarians and whether they are using them to their full potential. In 2001, the Hansard Society Commission on Parliamentary Scrutiny warned, when considering the potential advantages of RAB that 'unless MPs, and Commons' staff, are well trained and supported, there is the distinct possibility that all concerned will become even more confused'. The report argued:

The key to making best use of the benefits of resource accounting is the motivation of MPs, and the priorities they set for themselves, in the chamber and in committee. Improved accounts, more meaningful and open information, and training and support resources; all ultimately count for very little if MPs do not engage in the process.

12.7 In the five years since the full implementation of RAB it is not clear to what extent MPs have availed themselves of these opportunities. There is a danger that the same problems could apply to Whole of Government Accounts, which will be first published for the fiscal year 2006-07. **It is essential that Parliament responds by making full use of the information and opportunities presented by these innovations to strengthen its scrutiny work. We reiterate the Scrutiny Commission's recommendation for more training and support resources for MPs.** Ultimately, however, it is the culture of scrutiny that exists in Parliament as well as the motivation of individual MPs and peers that will dictate the way that Parliament responds to the various innovations that might improve government accountability.

Government data

12.8 The ability of the NAO and Parliament to scrutinise fully government expenditure is dependent on the quality – the accuracy, clarity and relevance – of the figures supplied by government, and the methods used to assess expenditure.

Recent evidence suggests a mixed picture in this area – the data used to measure the performance targets set out in PSAs have faced particular criticism.[67] In 2002 the NAO launched a programme to work with departments to identify ways in which they could strengthen their data systems, and in March 2006 published a report in which it found that 'variable' progress had been made in establishing 'robust' data systems.[68] The problem with the quality of data was reiterated in another recent NAO report on *Progress in Improving Government Efficiency*.[69] It found that reported efficiency gains (towards the government's £21.5 billion 'Gershon' efficiency target) may not be measured accurately, and should be considered provisional and subject to further verification.

12.9 Responding on behalf of the government, the then Treasury Minister Des Browne MP said that the government was 'dealing with the measurement issues' and would 'continue to report, in a transparent fashion, to Parliament and the country on the progress that we are making on this important matter'.[70] In addition, in March 2006 the Office for National Statistics published an article outlining the 'significant progress' already made in respect of the quality of public spending data.[71] **Given the huge importance of the quality of government data, we welcome such work by the NAO and would argue that more such work needs to be done. Parliament should play an active role in monitoring progress in this area.**

---

[67] PSAs are three year agreements negotiated between individual departments and the Treasury and are intended to indicate what is obtained for money spent.
[68] NAO (2005) *Public Service Agreements: Managing Data Quality – Compendium Report and National Audit Office* (2006) *Second validation compendium report: 2003-06 PSA data systems.*
[69] NAO (2005-06) *Progress in Improving Government Efficiency,* HC 802.
[70] House of Commons Hansard, 2 March 2006, Column 382.
[71] Office for National Statistics (2006) *Improving the Quality of Central Government Expenditure Data.*

Section 13

Support and Resources

13.1 It is unrealistic, and probably undesirable, to expect MPs and Peers to be technical experts. They are politicians and they alone have the unique ability to add political judgement to the research and evidence of others. However, they need access to this specialist information and research in order to make a political judgement. Select committees have long had designated staff (with a range of different expertises and skills) to support their work. In addition, MPs and Peers are able to draw on specialist support, including information and research, provided by subject analysts based in the libraries in the Commons and Lords.

13.2 In 2002, there was a major advance when the Scrutiny Unit (SU) was established in the Commons to provide greater assistance to select committees on a range of matters including financial scrutiny and pre-legislative scrutiny. The formation of the SU was part of a package of reforms introduced by Robin Cook when he was Leader of the House of Commons. He brought forward core objectives for the work of select committees (which included financial scrutiny) and the SU was established to help committees undertake this work. The Unit contains about 20 staff representing a mixture of different skills and a considerable part of its work relates to financial scrutiny, for example, providing briefings on estimate issues. It should be noted that the SU provides specialist support for select committees rather than for individual MPs.

13.3 It is difficult to quantify precisely the increased amount of financial scrutiny conducted by select committees. However, analysis of their work since the introduction of core objectives for select committees and the formation of the Scrutiny Unit suggests that it has had a positive impact. For example, in the 2004-05 parliamentary session, a greater number of select committees produced reports on expenditure related issues than had previously been the case. Greater use of internal parliamentary information and monitoring would improve the potential of follow-up work and shared information. The SU is able to take an overview of the quality of financial performance and reporting across the full range of government activity. This enables a more systematic appreciation by the House as a whole of the areas of good and bad practice and relative success in applying resources to achieve policy outcomes across the range of government departments. For individual committees to be able to use these wider findings in assessing the relative strengths and weaknesses of their particular department is a significant gain.

13.4 However, because of the SU focus on select committees, it appears that not all MPs know about its work. There has been progress on this front: it has been agreed that from June 2006 onwards all SU reports will be put on an external website. We welcome the moves to increase the profile of the Scrutiny Unit. **Another means to raise the SU's profile, and make its work more accessible to individual MPs as well as select committees, would be for it to produce a bulletin or digest on financial matters which could be circulated to all MPs.** The digest might include information on recent reports, follow-up or lack of it on PAC or select committee reports, external developments in the field, government activity, relevant statistics and so on. This would help all MPs to remain informed and aware of an issue long after the NAO, PAC or departmental select committees had reported. The information in such a digest would help to strengthen MPs' work, not only in committees and debates on the floor of the House, but also in their constituency work.

13.5 The success of the Scrutiny Unit in improving the quantity and quality of financial scrutiny provides a strong case that increased support and resources would improve Parliament's accountability functions yet further. **One option would be for the Liaison Committee to assess whether the SU should be expanded and whether extra staff would improve Parliament's financial scrutiny functions.** Another option was put forward by the Hansard Society Scrutiny Commission. **It proposed that a designated new body, the Parliamentary Finance Office, should be established to provide high quality research, access to specialist advice and expertise, support for collection and analysis of evidence and report drafting.** Its remit would be to support all financial functions of select committees, including work on estimates, scrutiny of government expenditure and analysis of spending outcomes. Additionally, Gwyneth Dunwoody MP has argued that 'The simplest and the most effective way of enabling Parliament to scrutinise such work would be for the House of Commons to create the equivalent of the American General Accounting Office' (now renamed the Government Accountability Office), which she described as:

An institution which originally began as an audit of government expenditure, but has developed into an information and support system for both the Senate and Congress, able to study government figures and check the assumptions on which many basic decisions have been made. It is answerable only to Parliament. The creation of such a unit would not only transform the work of Parliament but would enable it to check and evaluate Ministers' decisions more fully.

13.6 It is clear that many observers would endorse the call for improved support and expertise to be made available to Parliament. In fact, the establishment of the Scrutiny Unit has already provided a basic model, (albeit at present on a relatively small scale) for the sort of bodies outlined above, and it has played an important part in increasing financial expertise and giving the subject greater prominence within Parliament. The central question is whether a larger body, with more capacity and the potential for further detailed work, would enhance Parliament's ability to hold government to account in this area and whether individual parliamentarians would be willing to take on extra or different ways of working. **We recommend that the work of the Scrutiny Unit should be built upon, either through an expansion of its role or through its evolution into a Parliamentary Finance Office to provide comprehensive support on all financial matters to individual parliamentarians and select committees.**

Section 14

Connecting with the public

14.1 Parliament has a responsibility to members of the public to ensure that financial scrutiny (and its resulting impact on government finance) is carried out in the public interest and is reflective of its concerns. For Parliament to be able to carry out this role effectively, it is essential that the system is as transparent and accessible as possible. It is equally important that people who wish to contribute are able to have their say and that in carrying out its scrutiny work, Parliament takes into account the interests and concerns of different sections of society.

Accessibility and transparency

14.2 In recent years, declining voter turnout in elections has prompted fears about a 'crisis of democracy' and widespread political disengagement. While much of the debate has hovered around the question of support for political parties, Hansard Society research suggests that there is also a particular problem when it comes to perceptions of Parliament. The 2005 report of the Hansard Society Commission on the Communication of Parliamentary Democracy, chaired by Lord Puttnam concluded that this is partly a product of the way that Parliament presents itself to the public.[72] The report, *Parliament in the Public Eye*, identified a range of problems with Parliament's communication strategy. These included a failure to respond to the changing political context, link Parliament's work to wider political issues and make information about its work easily accessible to the public. This fuels the perception that Parliament is an inward looking institution, and contributes to public disengagement from it.

14.3 The problem is all the more acute on matters such as Parliament's financial scrutiny work. First, the complexity of the subject matter and procedures involved – a theme that has run through this report – makes it incomprehensible even for many Members of Parliament. As the Society of Welsh Treasurers noted in their evidence to this inquiry, 'it is difficult to see how the average Member of Parliament can be expected to understand this level of detail and effectively contribute to the debate'. There is also a problem of compartmentalisation: several participants at our seminar

---

[72] Hansard Society Commission on the Communication of Parliamentary Democracy, Chaired by David Puttnam (2005) *Members Only? Parliament in the Public Eye*, Hansard Society: London.

felt that finance was often treated as a subject that is completely separate to the rest of the work in Parliament, whereas in reality it is inextricably linked to all other aspects of policy. In order to engage MPs and the wider population, it is essential for Parliament to be seen to be making the link between finance and public policy and communicating the impact of its financial scrutiny work on people's lives and public service delivery. At one level this requires Parliament to incorporate coverage of financial matters into its own communication and media strategy so that this aspect of its work enters the public domain.

14.4 At the same time, it requires better information for MPs so that they are able to communicate this important aspect of Parliament's work to their constituents and the wider public. The Hansard Society Scrutiny Commission report pointed out that there is no single document that provides information on the various procedures involved in financial scrutiny and argued that the creation of such a document would help parliamentarians in their work and would also explain to the public the avenues to feed into the process. **We reiterate the proposal that Parliament should provide a document that clearly sets out the operation of parliamentary authorisation for government finance, as well as scrutiny and audit of government spending, which is publicly available (including on the parliamentary website). In addition, regular updates to parliamentarians by the Scrutiny Unit on Parliament's ongoing financial scrutiny work (a recommendation made in section 13) should also be made publicly available.** While it is likely and understandable that financial procedures will be of interest only to a small minority, and mostly to technical experts, it is nonetheless important for this material to be readily available and accessible.

Public involvement and representation

14.5 *Parliament in the Public Eye* also highlighted the dearth of opportunities for members of the public to contribute to the work of Parliament, noting 'where the public expect institutions to be responsive to their concerns, Parliament provides almost no opportunities for direct voter involvement, interaction or feedback'. On financial matters, select committees can provide the ideal forum for hearing the views and evidence of the public. Many organisations – covering a wide range of fields – have an interest in tax and spending issues (and their outcomes) and it is important that the views of civil society are able to inform the parliamentary process. In addition to expert bodies, **public consultation can help committees understand whether government policies are working, and what impact they are having on public services and on the lives of different sections of society.** In this sense public involvement is not just about offering opportunities for involvement, which members of the public have the right to expect; it is also about enabling Parliament to carry out its scrutiny work more effectively. As a World Bank Institute paper on gender budgeting notes:

By providing a platform for open discussion on the contents of the budget, legislatures can help to broaden and deepen public debate. Public hearings provide a structured way to bring into the budget debate the perspectives of experts from academia, civil society and the private sector. This can make the process more receptive to new concepts and approaches to budget such as gender analysis...[73]

14.6 Consultation with external bodies can also help ensure that government policies are reflective of the concerns of different sectors and sections of society. The Women's Budget Group argues that 'The UK Parliament can contribute significantly to ensuring a gender perspective is included in public expenditure', pointing to examples where work done by legislatures in France, South Africa and the devolved assemblies have, through work with external bodies, succeeded in incorporating gender budget analysis into their work. At a time of political disengagement, where there is cynicism about Parliament and politics, and where some sections of society feel alienated it is all the more important that the concerns of different groups are brought into Parliament's work. There is, of course, a danger that in creating new opportunities to hear directly from the public, more powerful organisations and interests, and those that shout the loudest, will dominate public consultations. **It is therefore essential for Parliament to have a strategy to actively engage more marginalised sections of society into its work in a way that does not undermine the fundamental representative system.**

---

[73] Wehner, J. and Byanyima, W. (ibid).

Section 15

Conclusion

15.1 Taxation and public spending underpin all forms of government activity. They go to the heart of politics and the relationship between government, Parliament and the public. The Hansard Society has had a long standing commitment to effective parliamentary democracy and in the 2001 report of our Commission on Parliamentary Scrutiny we identified financial scrutiny as a central component in enhancing the government's accountability to Parliament. One aspect of our work as a 'constructive friend' involves commending Parliament where its work and procedures are effective but also advocating changes where we believe that reforms could lead to improvements in the way that it holds government to account and connects with the public it represents.

15.2 In this report we have not set out to challenge the fundamentals of the United Kingdom's constitutional architecture or to question whether (or how) Parliament could occupy a different position in the political landscape. We have asked instead whether, when it comes to financial scrutiny, Parliament lives up to its constitutional expectations and fulfils its role as the publicly elected body charged with holding the government to account for its actions. Our answer is that in many areas Parliament performs its role as financial scrutineer reasonably effectively. We note, for example, that in examining past government expenditure Parliament does have a positive and important impact on the work of government, helping it to perform its role more effectively and efficiently. However, in many other areas, in particular the authorisation and scrutiny of government spending plans, there are significant gaps in the way that Parliament conducts its work. We argue, for example, that Parliament's influence over government spending proposals is virtually non existent and that all too often it simply acquiesces to requests from government, without sufficient scrutiny or debate. There has been some limited progress in this area, through the consideration of departmental reports by committees, but much more such work is needed.

15.3 The UK financial scrutiny system exists in sharp contrast to that in many other countries, including the US. Without calling for a move to a system such as that in the US – which would fundamentally alter the relationship between Parliament and Government – we argue that there should be more opportunities for meaningful parliamentary debate and consideration of government finance and greater openness and transparency from government about why choices are made. This should take place at as early a stage as is possible to enable Parliament's work to feed into the process by which government sets its spending and taxation plans. This is essential if Parliament is to provide authorisation and legitimacy to the work of government, obtain explanation and accountability about the actions of government and represent the views and concerns of the nation.

15.4 Parliament would also benefit from a more systematic approach to its scrutiny functions as a whole, which involves examining where scrutiny is needed, how it could be carried out, and how it can be evaluated properly. Using the example of scrutiny of PFI projects, we argue that changes in the way that government operates make it essential for Parliament to renew its ways of holding government to account on a regular basis. In the report we have outlined a range of procedural, structural and functional options for reform that would enable Parliament to carry out its role more effectively. At the same time, we have stressed that the reforms must be accompanied by a greater willingness from MPs and peers to conduct financial scrutiny work – both at a macro-level as well as the more detailed micro-level. Financial scrutiny should be considered as one of most vital roles of MPs, rather than as something to be left to technical experts. The specialist support and analysis provided to committees by the Scrutiny Unit, could be built on by developing the Unit into a Parliamentary Finance Office, which would support all financial functions of committees, as well as individual parliamentarians.

15.5 We have argued that particularly through more work by select committees, and supported by independent bodies and high quality research, Parliament can have a much greater impact on the work of government. Select committees, particularly the Treasury and Public Accounts Committees already undertake much good financial scrutiny work and have been joined by the Economic Affairs Committee in the Lords. There is, however, potential for much more work to be done by select committees within both Houses. A Finance and Audit Sub-Committee within each departmental select committee, for example, could give more thorough consideration to government estimates and spending plans, and follow up recommendations made by the PAC and the NAO to ensure that they are resulting in government action. This would also help ease the burdens on the PAC and the Treasury Committee and help them perform their roles more effectively. In particular, we are sure that there is significant potential for the work of the NAO/PAC to be more systematically followed up, and for greater monitoring of changes promised by the government to take place.

15.6 Even a small improvement in government efficiency and value for money would deliver significant savings for the public purse. Parliament and the audit bodies already play a part in identifying successes and failures and advocating improvements and efficiency savings. However, it is our contention that they could play a much more active role, especially in terms of follow-up of existing reports, to ensure that lessons are learnt and changes made.

15.7 We asked in our interim paper, 'Does Parliament improve government?' The answer is that it does, but with significant and undoubted limitations. Therefore, could it do more to live up to the constitutional expectations of it? It is our contention that it could, and it should. We hope that this report stimulates debate and encourages reform in this crucially important area.

Appendix 1: List of evidence received

1. Audit Commission
2. Centre for Public Scrutiny
3. The Chartered Institute of Public Finance and Accountancy
4. HM Treasury (on behalf of all government departments)
5. House of Commons Scrutiny Unit
6. National Audit Office
7. The Scottish Parliament
8. Society of Welsh Treasurers
9. Women's Budget Group
10. George Cunningham
11. Gwyneth Dunwoody MP
12. Lord Wakeham
13. David Walker, Editor, Public Magazine, *The Guardian*
14. Sir Nicholas Winterton MP

Appendix 2: List of attendees at the private seminar

This report draws on discussion that took place at a private seminar held by the Hansard Society on 13 December 2005 at PricewaterhouseCoopers, Embankment Place, London. The seminar was held under Chatham House Rules: as such no comments made during the discussion are attributable to any individual participant.

Chairman: Rt Hon the Lord Holme of Cheltenham, CBE (Chairman, Hansard Society and Chairman, House of Lords Constitution Committee)

Richard Bacon MP	Member, Public Accounts Committee
Mike Barnes	Head of Professional Support – Local Government, Audit Commission
Professor Vernon Bogdanor	Professor of Politics and Government, and Vice Principal, Brasenose College

Alex Brazier	Senior Research Fellow, Hansard Society
Joe Cavanagh	Director, Business Development, National Audit Office
Robert Chote	Director, Institute for Fiscal Studies
Steve Clark	Director, Government Financial Management, PricewaterhouseCoopers
Gillian Fawcett	Deputy Head of Finance, Scrutiny Unit, House of Commons
Alex Hardy	Communications Executive, Centre for Public Scrutiny
Colin Lee	Clerk to the Treasury Committee, House of Commons
Thomas Lewis	Head of Policy for Central Government, CIPFA
Lesley Lodge	Policy Manager, CIPFA
Dr Declan McHugh	Director, Parliament and Government Programme, Hansard Society
George Mudie MP	Member, Treasury Committee and former member, Public Accounts Committee
Vidya Ram	Project Manager, Parliament and Government Programme, Hansard Society
Peter Riddell	Chief Political Commentator, *The Times*
David Walker	Editor, Public Magazine, *The Guardian*

As part of this project, the authors of the report have also conducted a number of off-the-record interviews with individuals and organisations involved with financial scrutiny.

Bibliography

Blackburn, R. & Kennon, A. (2003) *Parliament: Functions, Practice and Procedures* (Sweet and Maxwell: London).

Brazier, A. (2006) *Scrutiny of European Union Business: Issues in Law Making Paper 8*; (2004) *Parliament, Politics and Law Making: Issues and Developments in the Legislative Process* and *Pre-Legislative Scrutiny: Issues in Law Making Paper 5*; (2003) *Parliament at the Apex: Parliamentary Scrutiny and Regulatory Bodies*; and (2000) *Parliament and the Public Purse: Improving Financial Scrutiny* and *Systematic Scrutiny, Reforming the Select Committees* (Hansard Society: London).

Brazier, A., Flinders, M. & McHugh, D. (2005) *New Politics, New Parliament? A review of parliamentary modernisation since 1997* (Hansard Society: London).

Chartered Institute of Public Finance and Accountancy (2001) *Introductory Guide to Central Government Finance and Financial Management*.

Conservative Party (2005) *The James Review of Tax Payer Value*.

Davey, E. (2000) *Making MPs work for our Money: Reforming Parliament's Role in Budget Scrutiny* (Centre for Reform: London).

Demirag, I., Dubnick, M. and Khadaroo, I. (2004) *Exploring the relationship between accountability and performance in the UK's Private Finance Initiative* (Queens University Belfast).

Elliot, M. and Rotherham, L, (2006) *The Bumper Book of Government Waste* (Harriman House: London).

Gay, O and Winetrobe, B. (2003) *Parliamentary Audit: The Audit Committee in Comparative Context*, report to the Audit Committee of the Scottish Parliament (Constitution Unit: University College London).

Hansard Society (2005) *Members Only? Parliament in the Public Eye: the report of the Hansard Society Commission on the Communication of Parliamentary Democracy*, chaired by David Puttnam and (2001) *The Challenge for Parliament: Making Government Accountable*, Report on the Commission on Parliamentary Scrutiny, chaired by Lord Newton of Braintree.

International Monetary Fund (1998) *Code of Good Practices on Fiscal Transparency* (IMF: Washington DC).

Jones, D. (2005) *UK Parliamentary Scrutiny of EU Legislation* (Foreign Policy Centre: London).

Kristensen, J.K., Groszyk, W.S. & Buhler, B (2002) 'Outcome focussed management and budgeting', *OECD Journal on Budgeting*, Vol 1, No. 4.

Lienert, I. (2005) *Who Controls the Budget: The Legislature or the Executive? International Monetary Fund (IMF) Working Paper* (IMF: Washington DC).

Lipsey, D. (2000) *Inside the Secret Treasury* (Penguin: London).

McEldowney, J. & Lee, C. (2005) 'Parliament and Public Money' in Giddings, P. (ed.) *The Future of Parliament: Chance or Decay?* (Palgrave: London).

McGee, D. G. (2002) *The Overseers: Public Accounts Committees and Public Spending* (Commonwealth Parliamentary Association: London).

Norton, P. (2005) *Parliament in British Politics* (London: Palgrave Macmillan); (1993) *Does Parliament Matter?* (Harvester Wheatsheaf: New York).

Reid, G. (1966) *The Politics of Financial Control: the Role of the House of Commons* (Hutchinson University Library: London).

Rogers, R. & Walters R. (2004) *How Parliament Works* (Pearson: London).

Schick, A. (2003) 'Can National Legislatures Regain an Effective Voice in Budget Policy?' *OECD Journal on Budgeting*, Vol. 1, No 3: pp. 15-42.

Shaoul, J. (2004) 'A critical appraisal of the private finance initiative: selecting a financial method or allocating economic wealth?', *Critical Perspectives on Accounting*.

Silk, P. & Walters, R. (1998) *How Parliament Works* (Longman: London).

Social Market Foundation (2005) *To the Point: A Blueprint for Good Targets,* Report of the Social Market Foundation Commission on the Use of Targets in Public Services.

Stapenhurst, R., et al. (2003) *Scrutinising Public Expenditures: Assessing the Performance of Public Accounts Committees* (World Bank Institute: Washington DC).

Stapenhurst, R. and Titsworth, J. (2001) 'Features and functions of supreme audit institutions', *World Bank PREM Note No. 59* (World Bank: Washington DC).

Tyrie, A. (2000) *Mr Blair's Poodle: An agenda for reviving the House of Commons* (Centre for Policy Studies: London).

Wehner, J. & Byanyima, W. (2004) *Parliament, the Budget and Gender* (World Bank Institute: Washington).

Wehner, J. (2003) 'Principles and Patterns of Financial Scrutiny: Public Accounts Committees in the Commonwealth', *Commonwealth and Comparative Politics,* Vol. 41, No. 3: 21-36.

Government and Parliamentary Publications

Audit Commission (2005) *CPAs - The Harder Test: single tier and county councils' framework for 2005.*

Audit Committee (2005) *Annual Report 2004-5 (*Scottish Parliament).

Cabinet Office (1999) *Modernising Government,* Cm 4310.

Defence Committee (2003-4) *Lessons from Iraq,* HC 57-I.

Education and Skills Committee (2004-5) *Public Expenditure on Education and Skills,* HC 168; *UK e-university,* HC 205.

Environment Transport and Regional Affairs Committee (1999-2000) *Audit Commission,* HC174-I.

Erskine May (2004) *Parliamentary Practice.* (edited by Hutton, M. et al).

European Court of Auditors, *Treaty Establishing the European Community.*

European Scrutiny Committee (2004-5) *The Work of the Committee in 2004,* HC 38-VI.

European Union Committee (2005-6) *The 2006 EC Budget,* HL 22; (2004-5) *Annual Report 2004,* HL 186.

Foreign Affairs Committee (2005-6) *Annual Report,* HC 903.

Gershon, P. (2004) *Releasing Resources to the Front Line: Independent Review of Public Sector Efficiency,* HM Treasury.

Gay, O. (2005) *The Lyons and Gershon Reviews and Variations in Civil Service Conditions,* House of Commons Library.

Home Affairs Committee (2004-5) *Work of the Committee in 2004-5,* HC 280.

House of Commons Library (2006) *Financial Procedure;* (2004) *The Public Audit (Wales) Bill: Research Paper 04/45;* (2003) *European Communities Legislation.*

Leaders Group on Working Practices, (2002) *Report by the Group Appointed to Consider how the Working Practices of the House can be Improved, and to make Recommendation,* HL 111.

Liaison Committee (2004-5) *Annual Report for 2004,* Appendix 4, HC 419.

Modernisation Committee (2004-05) Scrutiny of European Business, HC 465 I-II.

National Audit Office (2005-06) *Progress in Improving Government Efficiency,* HC 802.

National Audit Office/ Audit Commission (2005) *Delivery Chain Analysis for Bus Services in England.*

Northern Ireland Affairs Committee (2004-5) *Northern Ireland Department 2002-3 Resource Accounts,* HC 173.

Procedure Committee (2003-4) *Estimates and Appropriation Procedure,* HC 393; (1999 – 2000), *Government Response to the Sixth Report of Session 1998-99: Procedure for Debate on the Government's Expenditure Plans,* HC 388; (1998-99) *The Procedure for Debate on the Government's Expenditure Plans,* HC 295.

Public Accounts Committee (2005-6) *The BBC's White City 2 Development,* HC 652; (2004-5) *Financial Management of the European Union,* HC 498; *Managing Risk to Improve Public Services,* HC 444; *Improving Departments' Capability to Procure Cost-effectively,* HC 541; *Difficult Forms: How Government Departments Interact with Citizens,* HC 255; *Network Rail: Making a Fresh Start,* HC 556; *Ministry of Defence: The Rapid Procurement of Capability to Support Operations,* HC 70 and *Department of Health: Reforming NHS Dentistry,* HC 167; (2003-04) *Managing Resources to Deliver Better Public Services,* HC 181; (2000-1) *Review of Audit and Accountability for Central Government,* HC 260; and (1999-2000) *Government Resources and Accounts Bill,* HC 127.

Scottish Parliament Information Centre (2000) *The Annual Budgetary Process.*

Lord Sharman of Redlynch (2001) *The Review of Audit and Accountability for Central Government.*

Tax Law Review Committee (2003) *Making Tax Law: Report of a Working Party on the Institutional Processes for the Parliamentary Scrutiny of Tax Proposals and for the Enactment of Tax Legislation*, Chaired by Sir Alan Budd, TLRC Discussion Paper No. 3 (Institute for Fiscal Studies: London).

HM Treasury (2004) *Spending Review 2004*; and (2001) *Resource Accounting and Budgeting. A short guide to the financial reforms.*

Further publications from the HANSARD SOCIETY

Inside the Counting House: A discussion paper on Parliamentary Scrutiny of Government Finance
Alex Brazier and Vidya Ram
(ISBN 0 900432 92 6), £5, July 2005
Interim report of the Hansard Society's inquiry into financial scrutiny, which presents an accessible overview of the current system in Parliament, highlighting its strengths and weaknesses.

New Politics, New Parliament?: A review of parliamentary modernisation since 1997
(by Alex Brazier, Matthew Flinders and Declan McHugh)
(ISBN 0 900432 62 4), £10, June 2005
Report analysing the modernisation of parliamentary procedures and practices that have occurred since 1997, and exploring whether they have been successful in strengthening the role of Parliament and considering what future steps should be taken.

Parliament, Politics and Law Making: Issues and Developments in the Legislative Process
(edited by Alex Brazier)
(ISBN 0 900432 57 8), £20, December 2004
To follow up its influential 1992 report, *Making the Law*, the Hansard Society has published a collection of essays exploring recent issues and developments in the legislative process.

Making the Law: The Report of the Hansard Society Commission on the Legislative Process
(ISBN 0 900432 24 1), £16, 1992
An authoritative text on the UK legislative process whose recommendations have been extremely influential within Parliament and Government.

Parliament at the Apex: Parliamentary scrutiny and regulatory bodies
(Alex Brazier)
(ISBN 0 900432 96 9), £7.50, February 2003
This report looks at Parliament's relationship with regulatory bodies.

Publications can be ordered from hansard@hansard.lse.ac.uk
or 020 7438 1229 (fax)
or by post from
Hansard Society, 40-43 Chancery Lane, London WC2A 1JA.
For further information visit www.hansardsociety.org.uk